W9-BUC-084

Published in 2010 by Stewart, Tabori & Chang
An imprint of ABRAMS

Text copyright © 2010, Berroco, Inc.
Photographs copyright © 2010, Thayer Allyson Gowdy

All rights reserved. No portion of this book may be reproduced, stored in a
retrieval system, or transmitted in any form or by any means, mechanical,
electronic, photocopying, recording, or otherwise, without written permission
from the publisher.

Library of Congress Cataloging-in-Publication Data
Gaughan, Norah.
Comfort knitting & crochet : afghans / by Norah Gaughan, Margery Winter,
and the Berroco Design Team ; photographs by Thayer Allyson Gowdy.
     p. cm.
  ISBN 978-1-58479-826-2
 1. Afghans (Coverlets) 2. Knitting--Patterns. I. Winter, Margery. II.
Title.
  TT825.G283 2010
  746.43'0437--dc22
2009029918

Editor: Liana Allday
Designer: Onethread
Production Manager: Jacqueline Poirier

The text of this book was composed in Meta and News 702 BT.

Printed and bound in China
10 9 8 7 6 5 4 3 2 1

Stewart, Tabori & Chang books are available at special discounts when
purchased in quantity for premiums and promotions as well as fundraising
or educational use. Special editions can also be created to specification.
For details, contact specialsales@abramsbooks.com or the address below.

THE ART OF BOOKS SINCE 1949

115 West 18th Street
New York, NY 10011
www.abramsbooks.com

Those trademarks listed below and followed by ® are
registered trademarks of Berroco, Inc. in the United States.

BERROCO®
BERROCO COMFORT®
BERROCO COMFORT® CHUNKY
BERROCO COMFORT® DK

www.Berroco.com
info@berroco.com

COMFORT KNITTING & CROCHET
AFGHANS

MORE THAN 50 BEAUTIFUL, AFFORDABLE DESIGNS
FEATURING BERROCO'S COMFORT YARN

Norah Gaughan, Margery Winter, and the Berroco Design Team

Photographs by Thayer Allyson Gowdy
Styling by Karen Schaupeter

STC CRAFT / A MELANIE FALICK BOOK
STEWART, TABORI & CHANG
NEW YORK

knit

crochet

INTRODUCTION

something for everyone

For many of us, an afghan is the epitome of comfort. It is a staple of the home, the finishing touch that pulls together a living room or bedroom and makes it feel complete. But the usefulness of an afghan extends far beyond sofas and beds. An afghan easily transforms into a picnic blanket for a day at the beach, a wrap at dusk when the temperature drops, even a child's playtime tent.

The process of making an afghan is often as rewarding as the finished product, since there are so many opportunities to customize it to your personal taste and needs. Whether you are creating an afghan for yourself, as a housewarming gift, or to welcome a new baby into the world, the process is a creative meditation, and the result is a beautiful representation of time, skill, love, and good wishes.

In this book, you will find more than 50 knitted and crocheted afghans, each made with Berroco Comfort. Comfort is an ultra-soft blend of super fine acrylic and nylon, spun into a luxury twist usually reserved for the finest merino wools. It is hypoallergenic and can be machine-washed and -dried. Additionally, it is affordably priced and available in an exquisite range of more than 95 shades.

When we began to design this collection, we thought about the different types of homes people live in—from urban to rural, traditional to modern, and spare to embellished—and the types of afghans that would fit in them. We then sought further inspiration from textiles, crafts, and folk art around the world. For example, Houndstooth (page 60) and Herringbone (page 140) take their inspiration from traditional Scottish tweeds; Flokati (page 144) is a playful take on woolen rugs from Eastern Europe; and both Ethel (page 40) and Ukrainian Tiles (page 118) are derived from traditional folk crafts, Delft pottery and Ukrainian Easter Eggs, respectively. And of course, specialty knitting and crochet techniques are represented here as well. For example, Textured Knots (page 56) and Aran (page 149) showcase cables from the Aran Isles, and Irish Floral (page 62) is a modern representation of traditional Irish crochet.

The projects in *Comfort Knitting and Crochet: Afghans* are intended for every skill level, from beginner to advanced. And because making many of them involves repeating a stitch pattern or technique over and over, they are a perfect opportunity for learning and perfecting.

With so many options from which to choose, we hope that you will turn to this book for afghan ideas for many years to come.

Bicolor
Chevron

A tailored interpretation of a traditional chevron pattern, this afghan features micro-stripes created using two subtly contrasting yarn colors and single and half double crochet stitches. The gentle gradation of color produces a refined result reminiscent of Scottish tweeds.

Finished Measurements
45" wide x 60" long

Yarn
Berroco Comfort (50% super fine nylon / 50% super fine acrylic; 100 grams / 210 yards): 7 skeins #9720 Hummus (A); 9 skeins #9748 Aunt Martha Green (B)

Crochet Hook
Crochet hook size US H/8 (5 mm)
Change hook size if necessary to obtain correct gauge.

Notions
Stitch holders

Gauge
16 sts and 14 rows = 4" (10 cm) in Chevron Pattern

Stitch Pattern
CHEVRON PATTERN (multiple of 27 sts + 14 + ch1; 2-row repeat)
Set-Up Row: 2 hdc in 2nd ch from hook, hdc in next 5 ch, *sk 2 ch, 1 hdc in next 12 chs, 3 hdc in next ch, hdc in next 12 ch; repeat from * 7 times, end sk 2 ch, hdc in next 5 ch, 2 hdc in last ch. Do not turn. Do not cut yarn. Place last loop on a holder. Return to beginning of row.
Row 1: Change to B. 2 sc in first hdc, 1 sc in next 5 hdc, *sk 2 sts, 1 sc in next 12 hdc, 3 sc in next hdc, work 1 sc in next 12 hdc; repeat from * 7 times, end sk 2 sts, 1 sc in next 5 hdc, 2 sc in last hdc. Do not cut yarn. Place last loop on a holder. Turn.
Row 2: Place held loop (A) on hook. *2 hdc in first sc, hdc in next 5 sc, *sk 2 sc, 1 hdc in next 12 sc, 3 hdc in next sc, hdc in next 12 hdc; repeat from * 7 times, end sk 2 sts, hdc in next 5 sc, 2 hdc in last sc. Do not turn. Do not cut yarn. Place last loop on a holder. Return to beginning of row. Place held loop (B) on hook.
Repeat Rows 1 and 2 for Chevron Pattern.

Afghan
Using A, ch 231.
Begin Chevron Pattern; work even until piece measures 60" from the beginning. Fasten off.

Finishing
Block lightly (see Special Techniques, page 158).

Marrakesh

Named for the Moroccan city of Marrakesh, this coverlet reflects the city's exotic flavors and rich tones. The solid background is made using crocheted afghan stitch, which requires a particular long hook, and is then embellished with lanky folk art flowers. The monochromatic floral embroidery is a loose interpretation of the gold embroidery found on traditional caftans from the region.

Finished Measurements

45" wide x 60" long

Yarn

Berroco Comfort (50% super fine nylon / 50% super fine acrylic; 100 grams / 210 yards): 15 skeins #9724 Pumpkin (A)
Berroco Comfort Chunky (50% super fine nylon / 50% super fine acrylic; 100 grams / 150 yards): 2 skeins #5703 Barley (B)

Crochet Hook

Tunisian crochet hook size US H/8 (5 mm)
Change hook size if necessary to obtain correct gauge.

Gauge

18 sts and 32 rows = 4" (10 cm) in Tunisian Stitch, using A

Stitch Pattern

TUNISIAN STITCH (any number of sts; 2-row repeat)
Note: All rows are RS rows.
Set-Up Row: Insert hook in 2nd ch from the hook, yo and pull through, keeping the loop on the hook; repeat in each ch across. Do not turn.
Row 1: Working from left to right, ch 1, *yo and pull through the first 2 loops on the hook; repeat from * to end. Do not turn.
Row 2: Insert hook under the second single vertical thread, from right to left, yo and pull through, keeping the loop on the hook; repeat in each vertical thread to end. Do not turn.
Repeat Rows 1 and 2 for Tunisian Stitch.

Afghan

PANEL (make 3)
Using A, ch 65. Begin Tunisian st; work even until piece measures 60" from the beginning. Fasten off.

Finishing

Edging: Using A, work 1 row of sc across each side edge of each Panel. Join 3 Panels together as follows: Attach A to corner of first Panel, ch 2, sl st in corner of 2nd Panel, *ch 2, sk 1-2 edge sts, sl st in first Panel, ch 2, sk 1-2 edge sts, sl st in 2nd Panel, keeping Panels even; repeat from * to end. Join 2nd and 3rd Panels in same manner.
Embroidery: Using B, work embroidery following Diagrams. Block lightly (see Special Techniques, page 158).

EMBROIDERY DIAGRAM

KEY

✱ Straight St (p. 158)

Bouillon St Cluster (p. 157)

Roumanian St (p. 157)

Portuguese Stem St (below)

PORTUGUESE STEM ST

A   B   C   D   E   F

Retro

For Retro, we reached back in time and chose motifs that were all the rage twenty years ago, such as twisted-stitch mock cables, twisted-stitch blocks, and garter ribbing. Then we recombined these classics with a contemporary aesthetic in order to say something new.

Finished Measurements
46" wide x 54" long

Yarn
Berroco Comfort (50% super fine nylon / 50% super fine acrylic; 100 grams / 210 yards): 10 skeins #9713 Dusk

Needles
One pair straight needles size US 8 (5 mm)
One 29" (74 cm) long or longer circular (circ) needle size US 8 (5 mm)
Change needle size if necessary to obtain correct gauge.

Gauge
22 sts and 24 rows = 4" (10 cm) in pattern from Chart

Throw

COLUMN 1 (make 3)
Using straight needles, CO 40 sts. *Begin Chart; work Rows 1-26 twice, Rows 27-50 twice, then Rows 51-56 once. Repeat from * twice. BO all sts.

COLUMN 2 (make 2)
With straight needles, CO 40 sts. *Begin Chart; work Rows 27-50 twice, Rows 51-56 once, then Rows 1-26 twice. Repeat from * twice. BO all sts.

CHART

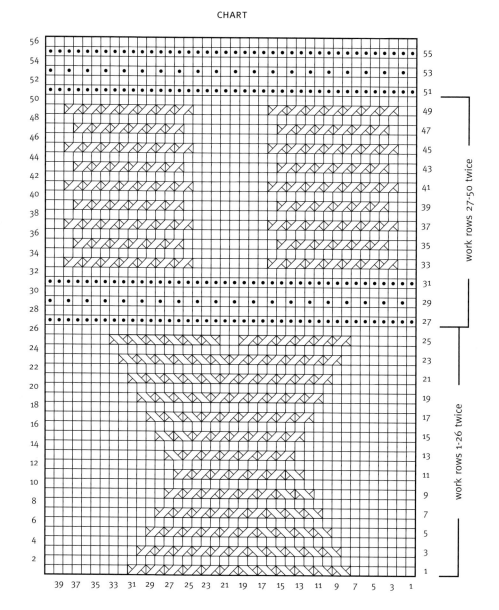

KEY

☐   Knit on RS, purl on WS.

⊡   Purl on RS, knit on WS.

⊠   Knit into back of second st, then knit first and second sts together through back loops, slip both sts from left-hand needle together.

⊠   K2tog, but do not drop sts from left-hand needle, insert right-hand needle between 2 sts just worked and knit first st again, slip both sts from left-hand needle together.

work rows 27–50 twice

work rows 1–26 twice

Finishing

Sew Columns together as follows: Column 1, 2, 1, 2, 1.

Side Edging: With RS facing, using circ needle, pick up and knit 220 sts evenly spaced along side edge of throw.

Row 1 (WS): K4, *p4, k4, repeat from * to end.

Row 2: Knit.

Repeat Rows 1 and 2 until Side Edging measures 3", ending with a WS row. BO all sts.

Repeat for second side of throw.

End Edging: With RS facing, using circ needle, pick up and knit 204 sts evenly spaced along end of throw. Work as for Side Edging. Repeat along second end of throw. BO all sts.

Block lightly (see Special Techniques, page 158).

Gypsy Patchwork

A wild patchwork quilt in bright hues evokes the gypsy in all of us. Patches of stranded colorwork are interspersed among easy seed-stitch squares and then embellished with relaxed, folkloric embroidery. The blocks are worked separately and then joined with bold, loose stitches. When assembled, this afghan is an explosion of cheerful color.

Finished Measurements

48" wide x 63" long

Yarn

Berroco Comfort (50% super fine nylon / 50% super fine acrylic; 100 grams / 210 yards): 8 skeins #9742 Pimpernel (B); 5 skeins each #9761 Lovage (A) and #9743 Goldenrod (C); 4 skeins #9725 Dutch Teal (D); 2 skeins #9745 Filbert (E)

Needles

One pair straight needles size US 9 (5.5 mm)
One pair straight needles size US 4 (3.5 mm)
Change needle size if necessary to obtain correct gauge.

Notions

Tapestry needle

Gauge

20 sts and 26 rows = 4" (10 cm) in Seed Stitch, using larger needles

Stitch Patterns

SEED STITCH (even number of sts; 2-row repeat)
Row 1: *K1, p1; repeat from * to end.
Row 2: *P1, k1; repeat from * to end.
Repeat Rows 1 and 2 for Seed Stitch.

MOSS STITCH (even number of sts; 4-row repeat)
Rows 1 and 2: *K1, p1; repeat from * to end.
Rows 3 and 4: *P1, k1; repeat from * to end.
Repeat Rows 1-4 for Moss Stitch.

Afghan

MOTIF A (make 28)
Using larger needles and A, CO 30 sts. Begin Seed st; work even for 30 rows. BO all sts.
Using tapestry needle and 2 strands of E held together, work Overcast st (see Special Techniques, page 157) evenly around the Motif.
Work embroidery following Motif A Chart.

MOTIF B (make 28)
Using larger needles and B, CO 30 sts. Begin Moss st; work even for 30 rows. BO all sts.
Using tapestry needle and 2 strands of E held together, work Overcast st evenly around the Motif.
Work embroidery following Motif B Chart.

MOTIF C (make 28)
Using larger needles and C, CO 30 sts. Begin Moss st; work even for 30 rows. BO all sts.
Using tapestry needle and 2 strands of A held together, work Overcast st evenly around the Motif.
Work embroidery following Motif C Chart.

MOTIF D (make 28)
Using larger needles and B, CO 29 sts. Begin Motif D Chart; work even until all 30 rows are completed. BO all sts.
Using tapestry needle and 2 strands of D held together, work Overcast st evenly around the Motif.

Finishing

Sew all Motifs together following Assembly Diagram, and working through Overcast sts.
Block lightly (see Special Techniques, page 158).

ASSEMBLY DIAGRAM

A	B	A	B	A	B	A	B
C	D	C	D	C	D	C	D
A	B	A	B	A	B	A	B
C	D	C	D	C	D	C	D
A	B	A	B	A	B	A	B
C	D	C	D	C	D	C	D
A	B	A	B	A	B	A	B
C	D	C	D	C	D	C	D
A	B	A	B	A	B	A	B
C	D	C	D	C	D	C	D
A	B	A	B	A	B	A	B
C	D	C	D	C	D	C	D
A	B	A	B	A	B	A	B
C	D	C	D	C	D	C	D

KEY

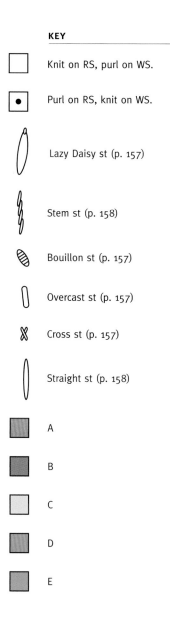

Knit on RS, purl on WS.

Purl on RS, knit on WS.

Lazy Daisy st (p. 157)

Stem st (p. 158)

Bouillon st (p. 157)

Overcast st (p. 157)

Cross st (p. 157)

Straight st (p. 158)

A

B

C

D

E

MOTIF A

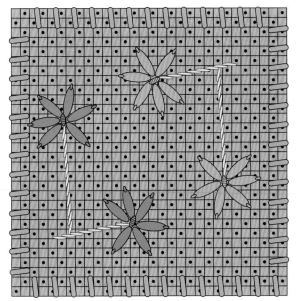

MOTIF B

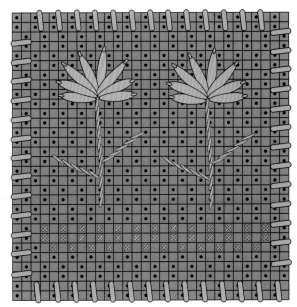

MOTIF C

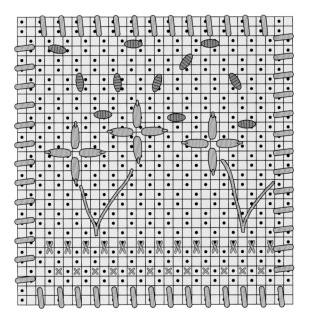

MOTIF D

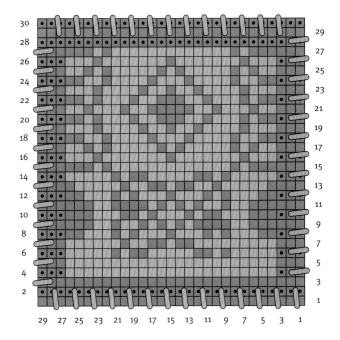

Bright Star

Inspired by the intricate piecing of patchwork quilts, the large, brightly colored stars in this afghan are mainly composed of mitered squares. Since the color changes within the squares are all in straight, intuitive lines, this is a perfect project on which to learn the art of intarsia. The straight lines also make the chart easy to memorize, so you can comfortably engage in conversation as you work.

Finished Measurements

50" wide x 60" long

Yarn

Berroco Comfort (50% super fine nylon / 50% super fine acrylic; 100 grams / 210 yards): 4 skeins each #9725 Dutch Teal (A), #9724 Pumpkin (B), and #9743 Goldenrod (C); 3 skeins each #9753 Aegean Sea (D) and #9717 Raspberry Coulis (E)

Needles

One pair straight needles size US 9 (5.5 mm)
Change needle size if necessary to obtain correct gauge.

Notions

Crochet hook size US H/8 (5 mm)

Gauge

18 sts and 17 rows = 4" (10 cm) in Garter stitch (knit every row)

Afghan

SQUARE A (make 16)
CO 22 sts A, 22 sts B, 22 sts C, then 22 sts A–88 sts.
Knit 1 row, changing colors as established.
Decrease Row 1 (RS): K21 A; k21, k2tog B; ssk, k21 C; k21 A–86 sts remain.
Knit 1 row, changing colors as established.
Decrease Row 2 (RS): K20 A; k21, k2tog B; ssk, k21 C; k20 A–84 sts remain.
Knit 1 row, changing colors as established.
Continue to work 1 less st at each side in A every RS row and AT THE SAME TIME, decrease 2 sts at center every RS row as established, work until no sts in A remain–22 sts in B and C remain. Change to D across all sts; continue to decrease 2 sts at center every RS row until 2 sts remain, ending with a RS row. K2tog. Fasten off remaining st.

NOTCHED SQUARE B (make 8)
Work as for Square 1 until no sts in A remain–22 sts in B and C remain. BO all sts.

SOLID SQUARES C (make 4)
Using E, CO 44 sts. Begin Garter st (knit every row); work even until piece measures 10" from the beginning, ending with a WS row. BO all sts.

SOLID RECTANGLES D (make 4)
Using E, CO 44 sts. Begin Garter st; work even until piece measures 5" from the beginning, ending with a WS row. BO all sts.

TOP RIGHT CORNER E
Using B, CO 22 sts. Knit 1 row.

Next Row (RS): K21 B; k1 A.
Knit 1 row, changing colors as established.
Next Row: K20 B; k2 A. Continue as established, working 1 less st in B and 1 more st in A every RS row until all sts are in A, ending with a WS row. BO all sts.

TOP LEFT CORNER F

Using C, CO 22 sts. Knit 1 row.
Next Row (RS): K1 A; k21 C.
Knit 1 row, changing colors as established.
Next Row: K2 A; k20 C.
Continue as established, working 1 more st in A and 1 less st in C every RS row until all sts are in A, ending with a WS row. BO all sts.

BOTTOM RIGHT CORNER G

Work as for Top Left Corner, reversing A and C.

BOTTOM LEFT CORNER H

Work as for Top Right Corner, reversing A and B.

CENTER SIDE RECTANGLES I (make 2)

Using A, CO 44 sts. Knit 1 row.
Next Row (RS): K1 B; k42 A; k1 C.
Knit 1 row, changing colors as established.
Next Row: K2 B; k40 A; k2 C.
Knit 1 row, changing colors as established.
Continue as established, working 1 more st with B and C every RS row until no sts A remain, ending with a WS row. BO all sts.

Finishing

Sew all pieces together following Assembly Diagram.
Edging: With RS facing, using crochet hook and D, work in sc around entire afghan, working 3 sc in each corner. Do not turn. Working from left to right, work in Reverse sc around entire afghan, working 3 Reverse sc in each corner, join with a sl st in first sc. Fasten off.
Block lightly (see Special Techniques, page 158).

Ribbon

This feminine throw is worked in a technique called broomstick lace. While technically crochet, broomstick lace is worked onto a very large knitting needle, which is less cumbersome than the tool originally used for the job—a broomstick. This stitch pattern works up very quickly into a distinctively pretty fabric that is subtly different on each side. We alternated panels with front and back sides facing out and then embellished the seams with an appliquéd cord of crab stitch crochet.

Finished Measurements
45" wide x 60" long

Yarn
Berroco Comfort (50% super fine nylon / 50% super fine acrylic; 100 grams / 210 yards): 13 skeins #9749 Aunt Abby Rose

Crochet Hook
Crochet hook size US H/8 (5 mm)
Change hook size if necessary to obtain correct gauge.

Needles
One straight needle size US 35 (19 mm)

Gauge
22 sts and 10 rows = 4" (10 cm) in Offset Broomstick Lace

Abbreviations
ELS (Extended Loop Stitch): With yarn in front, insert hook from back to front through st, yo, pull through, lengthen loop and slip it onto knitting needle.

LKS (Locking Stitch): Sl first st from needle to crochet hook, yo, pull up loop on hook 1", hold this loop steady with left hand, yo and draw through elongated st to make a 3rd strand the same length, insert hook into side of this 3rd elongated strand, yo and draw through loop, yo and draw through 2 loops on hook.

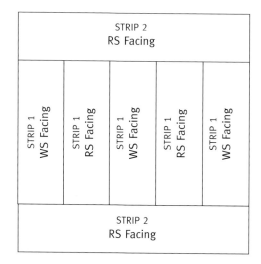

Stitch Pattern

OFFSET BROOMSTICK LACE (multiple of 6 sts + 1 ch; 4-row repeat)

Note: All rows are RS rows.

Set-Up Row: Sc in 2nd ch from hook, sc in each ch to end, do not turn.

Row 1: Ch 1, lengthen loop on hook and slip onto knitting needle, working from left to right, skip first sc, *1 ELS in each sc across, do not turn.

Row 2: LKS in first st, insert hook through next 5 loops on needle together, yo, pull through 5 loops on hook slipping loops from needle, yo, pull through 2 sts on hook to finish first sc, work 4 more sc in same space, *insert hook through next 6 loops together, yo, pull through 6 loops, slipping loops from needle, yo, pull through 2 sts on hook to complete first sc, work 5 more sc in same space; repeat from * to end, do not turn.

Row 3: Repeat Row 1, working last ELS in LKS.

Row 4: LKS in first loop on hook, insert hook through next 2 loops on needle together, yo, pull through 2 loops on hook, slipping loops from needle, yo, pull through 2 sts on hook, to finish first sc, work 1 more sc in same space, *insert hook through next 6 loops together, yo, pull through 6 loops, slipping loops from needle, yo, pull through 2 sts on hook to complete first sc, work 5 more sc in same space; repeat from * to last 3 loops, insert hook through last 3 loops together, yo, pull through 3 loops on hook, slipping loops from needle, yo, pull through 2 sts on hook to complete first sc, work 2 more sc in same space, do not turn.

Repeat Rows 1–4 for Offset Broomstick Lace.

Throw

STRIP 1 (make 5)

Ch 49. Begin Offset Broomstick Lace; work even until Strip measures 42" from the beginning.

STRIP 2 (make 2)

Ch 49. Begin Offset Broomstick Lace; work even until Strip measures 45" from the beginning.

Finishing

Sew Strips together following Assembly Diagram

Short Seam Coverings: (make 5)

Ch 150. Work Reverse sc along ch, then turn and work down the other side of ch. Fasten off. Sew over seams with a running st.

Long Seam Coverings: (make 2)

Ch 160. Work Reverse sc along ch, then turn and work down the other side of ch. Fasten off. Sew over seams with a running st.

Edging: With RS facing, work sc around entire throw, join with a sl st in first sc. Do not turn. Working from left to right, work in Reverse sc around entire throw, join with a sl st in first sc. Fasten off.

Block lightly (see Special Techniques, page 158).

Greenway

Color therapists tout green as the most restful color. With that in mind, we aimed for the ultimate in restfulness with this afghan, combining four shades of green with a neutral. Two rows of crocheted cluster stitch combine to form pretty, daisy-shaped blocks of color, with each daisy fitting neatly into the next.

Finished Measurements
45" wide x 60" long

Yarn
Berroco Comfort (50% super fine nylon / 50% super fine acrylic; 100 grams / 210 yards): 4 skeins #9748 Aunt Martha Green (B); 3 skeins each #9703 Barley (A), #9721 Sprig (C), and #9744 Teal (D); 2 skeins #9762 Spruce (E)

Crochet Hook
Crochet hook size US G/6 (4 mm)
Change hook size if necessary to obtain correct gauge.

Gauge
20 sts and 9 rows = 4" (10 cm) in Harlequin Pattern

Stitch Patterns
HARLEQUIN PATTERN (multiple of 8 sts + 1; 4-row repeat)
Note: Stitch pattern is reversible; there is no RS or WS.
Set-Up Row: [3 dc, ch 1, 3 dc] in 5th ch from hook, skip 3 ch, sc in next ch, *skip 3 ch, [3 dc, ch 1, 3 dc] in next ch, skip 3 ch, sc in next ch; repeat from *, turn.
Row 1: Ch 3, skip first sc, 3 dc-tog over next 3 dc, *ch 7, skip 1 ch, 6 dc-tog over next 6 dc (skipping sc in center); repeat from *, ending ch 7, skip 1 ch, 3 dc-tog over last 3 dc, dc in ch 1, turn.

Row 2: Ch 3, skip first dc, 3 dc in top of 3 dc-tog, *sc in ch 1 sp two rows below, enclosing the ch 7, [3 dc, ch 1, 3 dc] in top of 6 dc-tog; repeat from *, ending sc in ch 1 sp two rows below, enclosing the ch 7, 3 dc in top of 3 dc-tog, dc in 3rd of ch 3, turn.
Row 3: Ch 4, skip first dc, *6 dc-tog over next 6 dc (skipping sc in center), ch 7, skip 1 ch; repeat from *, ending 6 dc-tog (skipping sc in center), ch 3, sc in top of ch 3, turn.
Row 4: Ch 1, skip first sc and ch 3, *[3 dc, ch 1, 3 dc] in top of 6 dc-tog, sc in ch 1 sp 2 rows below, enclosing the 7 ch; repeat from *, ending [3 dc, ch 1, 3 dc] in top of 6 dc-tog, sc in 1st of ch 4, turn.
Repeat Rows 1-4 for Harlequin Pattern.

STRIPE SEQUENCE
Work 2 rows each in, *B, C, D, E, D, C, B, then A; repeat from * for Stripe Sequence.

Throw
Using A, ch 225. Begin Harlequin Pattern; work Set-Up Row. Contining Harlequin Pattern, begin Stripe Sequence; work even until piece measures approximately 60" from the beginning, ending with Row 4 and A. Fasten off.

Finishing
Edging: With RS facing, using A, work in sc around entire throw, join with a sl st in first sc. Working from left to right, work in Reverse sc around entire throw, join with a sl st in first Reverse sc. Fasten off.
Block lightly (see Special Techniques, page 158).

Fish Ripples

The colorful undulations of this crocheted baby blanket are reminiscent of schools of small fish swimming in the ocean. The stitch pattern works up extremely quickly, and the vivid stripes keep you eager to see more. Bright colors are perfect for a modern baby's room, and are likely to be loved long into childhood (and maybe into adulthood, too).

Finished Measurements

30" wide x 36" long

Yarn

Berroco Comfort (50% super fine nylon / 50% super fine acrylic; 100 grams / 210 yards): 1 skein each #9761 Lovage (A), #9724 Pumpkin (B), #9717 Raspberry Coulis (C), #9740 Seedling (D), #9725 Dutch Teal (E), and #9730 Teaberry (F)

Crochet Hook

Crochet hook size US G/6 (4 mm)
Change hook size if necessary to obtain correct gauge.

Gauge

15 sts and 14 rows = 4" (10 cm) in Fish Ripple Pattern

Stitch Patterns

FISH RIPPLE PATTERN (multiple of 16 sts + 2; 8-row repeat)

Note: Stitch Pattern is reversible; there is no RS or WS.

Set-Up Row: Sc in 2nd ch from hook, *sc in next ch, ch 1, skip 1 ch, hdc in next ch, ch 1, skip 1 ch, dc in next ch, [ch 1, skip 1 ch, tr in next ch] twice, ch 1, skip 1 ch, dc in next ch, ch 1, skip 1 ch, hdc in next ch, ch 1, skip 1 ch, sc in next ch, ** ch 1, skip 1 ch; repeat from *, ending last repeat at **, sc in last ch, turn.

Rows 1 and 5: Ch 1, sc in each st and ch-1 sp, turn.
Rows 2 and 6: Ch 1, sc in each sc across, turn.
Rows 3 and 4: Ch 4 (counts as tr), skip first st, *tr in next st, ch 1, skip 1 st, dc in next st, ch 1, skip 1 st, hdc in next st, [ch 1, skip 1 ch, sc in next st] twice, ch 1, skip 1 st, hdc in next st, ch 1, skip 1 st, dc in next st, ch 1, skip 1 st, tr in next st, **, ch 1, skip 1 st; repeat from *, ending last repeat at **, 1 tr in last st, turn.
Rows 7 and 8: Ch 1, 1 sc in first st, *sc in next st, ch 1, skip 1 st, hdc in next st, ch 1, skip 1 st, dc in next st, [ch 1, skip 1 st, tr in next st] twice, ch 1, skip 1 st, dc in next st, ch 1, skip 1 st, hdc in next st, ch 1, skip 1 st, sc in next st **, ch 1, skip 1 st; repeat from *, ending last repeat at **, sc in last st, turn, ch 1.
Repeat Rows 1-8 for Fish Ripple Pattern.

STRIPE SEQUENCE
Work 2 rows each in *B, C, D, E, F, then A; repeat from * for Stripe Sequence

Blanket

Using A, ch 114. Begin Fish Ripple Pattern; work Set-Up Row. Continuing in Fish Ripple Pattern, begin Stripe Sequence; work even until piece measures approximately 36" from the beginning, ending with Row 7 of Fish Ripple Pattern. Fasten off.

Finishing

Edging: Using A, work 1 row sc evenly along both side edges of blanket.
Block lightly (see Special Techniques, page 158).

Seersucker

The look of seersucker is distinctive and versatile, reminiscent of both baby rompers from the Sixties and the once-ubiquitous men's summer suit. But in this afghan, it is reproduced in a modern context with an irresistibly puckered texture. Who knew that the simple acts of increasing and decreasing could produce such an interesting result?

Finished Measurements
54" wide x 72" long

Yarn
Berroco Comfort (50% super fine nylon / 50% super fine acrylic; 100 grams / 210 yards): 22 skeins #9748 Aunt Martha Green

Needles
One pair straight needles size US 8 (5 mm)
Change needle size if necessary to obtain correct gauge.

Gauge
18 sts and 24 rows = 4" (10 cm) in Stockinette stitch (St st)

Afghan
SQUARE (make 48)

Section 1
CO 20 sts
Rows 1 (WS)-5: Work in St st, beginning with a purl row.
Row 6: *K1-f/b; repeat from * to end–40 sts.
Rows 7-11: Work in St st.
Row 12: *K2tog; repeat from * to end–20 sts remain.
Rows 13-24: Repeat Rows 1-12.
Rows 25-27: Work in St st.
BO all sts. Do not cut yarn.

Sections 2, 3, and 4
With RS of previous piece facing, pick up and knit 20 sts evenly spaced along left edge of previous piece. Work Rows 1-27 of Section 1. BO all sts. Do not cut yarn.

Sew Section 4 to Section 1 to form a Square.

Finishing
Sew Squares together so that afghan is 6 Squares wide by 8 Squares long.

Block lightly (see Special Techniques, page 158).

Weave

Though this afghan appears to have been made of long strips woven together like the reeds of a basket, each square is actually worked individually and sewn together at the end. The ribbed squares are ideal to make during social knit nights when concentration isn't required, while the more complicated cabled squares can be reserved for quieter times.

Finished Measurements
48" wide x 54" long

Yarn
Berroco Comfort (50% super fine nylon / 50% super fine acrylic; 100 grams / 210 yards): 17 skeins #9745 Filbert

Needles
One pair straight needles US 8 (5 mm)
Change needle size if necessary to obtain correct gauge.

Notions
Crochet hook size US H/8 (5 mm); cable needle (cn)

Gauge
26 sts and 26 rows = 4" (10 cm) in Weave Pattern from Chart

Stitch Pattern
2X2 RIB (multiple of 4 sts + 2; 2-row repeat)
Row 1 (RS): K2, *p2, k2; repeat from * to end.
Row 2: P2, *k2, p2; repeat from * to end.
Repeat Rows 1 and 2 for 2x2 Rib.

Afghan
CABLED SQUARE A (make 25)
CO 46 sts. Begin Weave Pattern from Chart; work even until piece measures 7" from the beginning, ending with a WS row. BO all sts.

RIBBED SQUARE B (make 24)
CO 46 sts. Begin 2x2 Rib; work even until piece measures 7" from the beginning, ending with a WS row. BO all sts in pattern.

CABLED TRIANGLE C (make 10)
CO 46 sts. Begin Weave Pattern from Chart; work even for 2 rows.

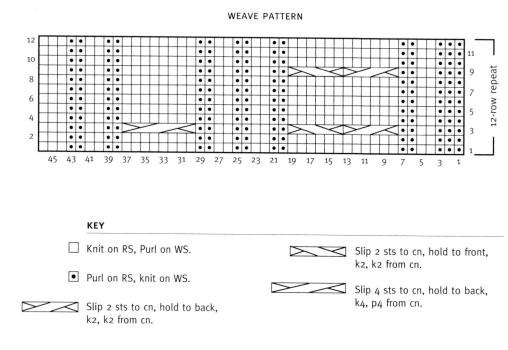

KEY

☐ Knit on RS, Purl on WS.

⊡ Purl on RS, knit on WS.

⬚ Slip 2 sts to cn, hold to back, k2, k2 from cn.

⬚ Slip 2 sts to cn, hold to front, k2, k2 from cn.

⬚ Slip 4 sts to cn, hold to back, k4, p4 from cn.

Shape Triangle

Decrease Row 1 (RS): Continuing with Weave Pattern, p2, ssk, work to end–45 sts remain.

Decrease Row 2 (WS): Work to last 4 sts, p2tog-tbl, k2–44 sts remain.

Repeat Decrease Rows 1 and 2 until 2 sts remain. Fasten off.

RIBBED TRIANGLE D (make 12)

CO 46 sts. Begin 2x2 Rib; work even for 2 rows.

Shape Triangle

Decrease Row 1 (RS): Continuing with 2x2 Rib, k2, ssk, work to end–45 sts remain.

Decrease Row 2 (WS): Work to last 4 sts, p2tog-tbl, p2–44 sts remain.

Repeat Decrease Rows 1 and 2 until 2 sts remain. Fasten off.

Finishing

Sew Squares and Triangles together following Assembly Diagram.

Edging: With RS facing, using crochet hook, join yarn at corner and work sc around entire piece (working 3 sc in each corner), join with a sl st in first sc. Working from left to right, work Reverse sc around entire piece (working 3 sc in each corner), join with a slip st in first sc. Fasten off.

Block lightly (see Special Techniques, page 158).

ASSEMBLY DIAGRAM

Dots

In the version of Dots shown here, we kept the palette soothing and feminine, though there is no limit to the number of color combinations that would work equally well. Think rich multitones on black for a stained-glass effect, soft blues and greens to mimic the look of sea glass, or all red dots on ecru for a retro feel. The solid dots are surrounded by a lacy filet mesh, against which the solid dots pop.

Finished Measurements
45" wide x 60" long

Yarn
Berroco Comfort (50% super fine nylon / 50% super fine acrylic; 100 grams / 210 yards): 8 skeins #9703 Barley (MC); 3 skeins each #9728 Raspberry Sorbet (B) and #9748 Aunt Martha Green (C); 2 skeins #9717 Raspberry Coulis (A)

Crochet Hook
Crochet hook size US H/8 (5 mm)
Change hook size if necessary to obtain correct gauge.

Gauge
1 Crocheted Dot = 4½" (11.5 cm) diameter

Throw
Note: Throw is worked by joining each Dot on last round to surrounding dots. Work from Assembly Diagram to determine which color Dot to work next.
Beginning at lower right-hand edge, work Dot C. Work Dot B, attaching to left edge of Dot C on Rnd 5 as described in Joining Rnd 5. Continue attaching on Rnd 5 to surrounding Dots.

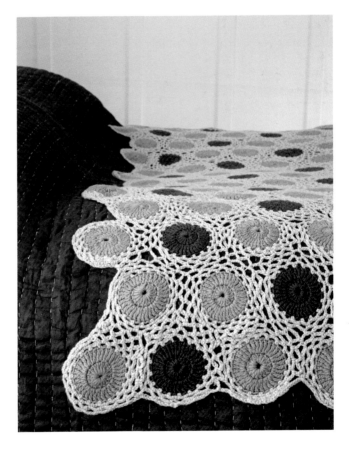

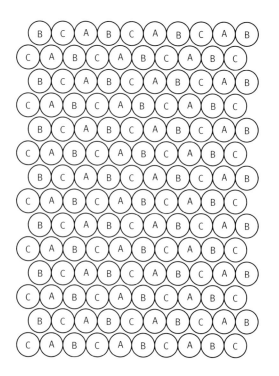

DOT C (make 42)

Using C, ch 10, join with a sl st to form ring.

Rnd 1: Ch 3 (counts as 1 dc), 16 dc in ring, join with a sl st in top of beginning ch-3–17 sts.

Rnd 2: Ch 4 (counts as 1 tr), tr in sl st of previous rnd, *2 tr in next dc; repeat from * around, join with a sl st in top of beginning ch-4–34 sts. Fasten off.

Rnd 3: With RS facing, join MC with a sl st in any tr. Sc in same tr, ch 3, *skip tr, sc in next tr, ch 3; repeat from * around, join with a sl st in first sc.

Rnd 4: Sl st into next ch-3 space, sc in same space, ch 4, *skip 1 sc, sc in next ch-3 space, ch 4; repeat from * around, join with a sl st in first sc.

Rnd 5: Sl st into next ch-4 space, sc in same space, ch 5, *skip 1 sc, sc in next ch-4 space, ch 5; repeat from * around, join with a sl st in first sc. Fasten off.

Joining Rnd 5: Instead of ch 5, work ch 2, attach to adjacent dot with sc, ch 2. Attach 2-3 times for each Dot, keeping joinings as "square" as possible.

DOT B (make 49)

Using B, work Rnds 1-2 as for Dot C, complete Rnds 3-5 with MC.

DOT A (make 49)

Using A, work Rnds 1-2 as for Dot C, complete Rnds 3-5 with MC.

Finishing

Block lightly (see Special Techniques, page 158).

Serpentine

Though this afghan is worked in just one neutral color, the textures make it visually thrilling. The highly dimensional ruffles are reminiscent of forms found in nature, from coral reefs to kale and lettuce leaves to the S-shaped curves of snakes. To accomplish this effect, flat panels of double crochet are punctuated with more ornate strips of treble crochet that coil around a mesh stitch base.

Finished Measurements

45" wide x 60" long

Yarn

Berroco Comfort (50% super fine nylon / 50% super fine acrylic; 100 grams / 210 yards): 21 skeins #9703 Barley

Crochet Hook

Crochet hook size US F/5 (3.75 mm)
Change hook size if necessary to obtain correct gauge.

Gauge

18 sts and 10 rows = 4" (10 cm) in Double Crochet (dc)

Afghan

WIDE STRIP (make 2)
Ch 57.
Set-Up Row: Dc in 4th ch from hook and in each ch across– 55 sts.
All Rows: Ch 3 (counts as dc), skip first dc, dc in each dc across, turn.
Work even until piece measures 60" from the beginning. Fasten off.

NARROW STRIP (make 2)
Ch 30.
Set-Up Row: Dc in 4th ch from hook and in each ch across–27 sts.
All Rows: Ch 3 (counts as dc), skip first dc, dc in each dc across, turn.
Work even until piece measures 60". Fasten off.

RUFFLED STRIP (make 3)
Ch 273.
Row 1: Dc in 6th ch from hook (counts as dc, ch 2, dc), *ch 2, skip 2 ch, dc in next ch; repeat from * to end, turn.
Row 2: Ch 5 (counts as dc and ch 2), skip 1st dc, dc in next dc, *ch 2, skip 1 dc, dc in next dc; repeat from * to end, turn.
Row 3: Repeat Row 2.
Row 4: Ch 4 (counts as tr), work 4 tr over first ch-2 sp, *turn work slightly to the left and work 5 tr over post of next dc, turn work slightly to the left and work 5 tr in ch-2 sp of row below, turn work slightly to the right and work 5 tr over post of next dc, turn work slightly to the right and work 5 tr in next ch-2 sp; repeat from * to end. Turn and work Row 4 along Row 2, then along Row 1. Fasten off.

Finishing

Sew Strips together in the following order: Narrow, Ruffled, Wide, Ruffled, Wide, Ruffled, Narrow.
Block lightly (see Special Techniques, page 158).

Ethel

The colors in this coverlet are reminiscent of traditional blue-and-white Delftware pottery from Holland. The circular motifs enhance the illusion by echoing the shape of saucers and plates. Two sizes of circles are joined together, leaving open spaces between, which creates a stunning effect when spread across a white comforter.

Finished Measurements
55" wide x 72" long

Yarn
Berroco Comfort DK (50% super fine nylon / 50% super fine acrylic; 50 grams / 178 yards): 17 skeins #2703 Barley (A); 9 skeins #2747 Cadet (B)

Crochet Hook
Crochet hook size US F/5 (3.75 mm)
Change hook size if necessary to obtain correct gauge.

Gauge
1 Large Circle = 5¼" (13.5 cm) circumference

Afghan
SMALL CIRCLE (make 88)
Using A, ch 5, sl st to form ring.
Rnd 1: Work ch 1, 9 sc into ring, end sl st into first sc.
Rnd 2: Change to B, ch 3, 1 dc in same sp, 2 dc in each sc around, end sl st in top of ch 3.
Rnd 3: Change to A, ch 1, 2 sc in same sp, 2 sc in each dc around, end sl st in first sc.
Rnd 4: Ch 1, sc in same sp, ch 3, skip 1 sc, sc in next sc; repeat from * around, end sl st in first sc. Fasten off.

KEY

○ Small Circle

◯ Large Circle

LARGE CIRCLE (make 108)

Note: Afghan is worked by joining each Large Circle on last round to surrounding Circles. Work from Assembly Diagram to determine placement of Circles.

Using B, ch 5, sl st to form ring.

Rnd 1: Work ch 1, 9 sc into ring, end sl st into first sc.

Rnd 2: Change to A, ch 3 (counts as dc), 1 dc in same sp, 2 dc in each sc around, end sl st in top of ch 3–18 sts.

Rnd 3: Change to B, ch 1, 2 sc in same sp, 2 dc in each dc around, end sl st in first sc–36 sts.

Rnd 4: Change to A, ch 3 (counts as dc), dc in next sc, 2 dc in next sc, *dc in next 2 sc, 2 dc in next sc; repeat from * around, end sl st in top of ch-3–48 sts.

Rnd 5: Change to B, ch 1, sc in same sp, sc in each dc around, end sl st in first sc.

Rnd 6: Using B, ch 3 (counts as dc), alternating colors A and B for each dc, dc in next 2 sc, 2 dc in 1 sc, *dc in next 3 sc, 2 dc in next sc; repeat from * around, end sl st in top of ch-3–60 sts.

Rnd 7: Change to A, ch 1, sc in same sp, sc in each dc around, end sl st in first sc.

Rnd 8: Using B, ch 3 (counts as dc), [work next 5 dc in colors A, B, A, 2B], *[repeating colors 1A, 1B, 1A, 1B, 2A, ** 1B, 1A, 1B, 1A, 2B], dc in next 4 sc, 2 dc in next sc; repeat from * around, ending at **, end sl st in top of ch-3–72 sts.

Rnd 9: Change to A, ch 1, sc in same sp, sc in each dc around.

Rnd 10 (worked on first Large Circle only): Ch 1 sc in same sp, *ch 3, skip 1 sc, sc in next sc; repeat from * around, end sl st in first sc.

Joining Rnd 10 (worked on all but first Large Circle): Ch 1, sc in same sp, join Circles over ch-3 sp of adjacent Circle as follows: [ch 2, sl st in ch-3 space on adjacent Circle, ch 2, skip 1 sc, sc in next sc on first Circle] twice, skipping 2-3 loops between joining Circles. Continue to join all Circles in this manner, following Assembly Diagram.

Finishing

Block lightly (see Special Techniques, page 158).

Spiral

This design borrows directly from traditional patchwork quilts, using a pattern that some quilters call a cat's tail and others know as snail's trail. Each square begins at the center with two colors and a tight spiral of single crochet; as the square is worked outward, the spirals grow larger and the colors twist around each other. When the squares are joined, they become vibrant whirlwinds. The entire afghan is created with a single stitch, using one color of yarn at a time, yet the results are mesmerizing.

Finished Measurements
36" wide x 45" long

Yarn
Berroco Comfort (50% super fine nylon / 50% super fine acrylic; 100 grams / 210 yards): 5 skeins each #9712 Buttercup (A) and #9721 Sprig (B)

Crochet Hooks
Crochet hook size US H/8 (5 mm)
Crochet hook size US I/9 (5.5 mm)
Change hook size if necessary to obtain correct gauge.

Gauge
14 sts and 18 rows = 4" (10 cm) in Single Crochet (sc), using smaller crochet hook

Special Stitches
Decrease 1: Pull up a loop in each of the next 2 sc, yo and pull through all loops on hook–1 sc decreased
Decrease 2: Pull up a loop in each of the next 3 sc, yo and pull through all loops on hook–2 sc decreased

Afghan

SQUARE (make 20)

Note: Each time you complete a rnd of triangles, the piece will be square.

Using smaller crochet hook and A, ch 6, join with a sl st to form a ring.

Rnd 1: Ch 2 (counts as 1 hdc), work dc, tr, dc, hdc in ring (triangle made), change to B and *work hdc, dc, tr, dc, hdc in ring (second triangle made), * change to A and repeat from * to *, change to B and repeat from * to *, join with a sl st in top of beginning ch-2–4 triangles made. Fasten off.

Rnd 2: With RS facing, join A with a sl st in center tr of A section of Rnd 1. Ch 1 (counts as 1 sc), work hdc in next dc, dc in next hdc, tr in space between triangles of Rnd 1, dc in next hdc, hdc in next dc, sc in center tr (triangle made), change to B and *work sc in same tr, hdc in next dc, dc in next hdc, tr in space between triangles of Rnd 1, dc in next hdc, hdc in next dc, sc in center tr *, change to A and repeat from * to *, change to B and repeat from * to *–4 triangles made. Fasten off.

Rnd 3: Begin in center tr of triangle worked with A on Rnd 2. With RS facing, using A, work 1 sc each in tr, dc, hdc, sc of that triangle, 1 sc between triangles, then 1 sc each in sc, hdc, dc and tr of next triangle–9 sc. Turn. *Decrease 1, sc to last 2 sc, decrease 1. Turn. Repeat from * until 3 sc remain. Turn. Decrease 2 (triangle made). Working in this manner, make 3 more triangles, with B, A, then B.

Rnd 4: Begin in center of triangle worked with A on Rnd 3. With RS facing, using A, work 5 sc across side of that triangle, 1 sc between triangles, 5 sc along side of next triangle–11 sc. Complete triangles as on Rnd 3. Make 3 more triangles with B, A, then B.

Change to larger crochet hook.

Rnd 5: Begin in center of triangle worked with A on Rnd 4. With RS facing, using A, work 6 sc across side of that triangle, 1 sc between triangles, 6 sc along side of next triangle–13 sc. Complete triangles as on Rnd 3. Make 3 more triangles with B, A, then B.

Rnd 6: Begin in center of triangle worked with A on Rnd 5. With RS facing, using A, work 9 sc along side of that triangle, 1 sc between triangles, 9 sc along side of next triangle–19 sc. Complete triangles as on Rnd 3. Make 3 more triangles with B, A, then B.

Finishing

Sew Squares together following Assembly Diagram.
Block lightly (see Special Techniques, page 158).

ASSEMBLY DIAGRAM

Basketweave

Knit and purl are all you need to create this elegant basketweave stitch. Basic, but not boring, this is the kind of knitting that flies by when you're watching a marathon of great old movies. This afghan is worked in one piece and requires no edging, so when you're done, you're done. The size shown here is big enough to top a double bed or completely cover you on the couch; we've also included instructions for a smaller, throw-sized version.

Finished Measurements
Afghan: 63" wide x 72" long
Throw: 45" wide x 55" long
Note: Numbers for Afghan are given first, and numbers for Throw are given in parentheses. Where only one number is given, it applies to both sizes.

Yarn
Berroco Comfort Chunky (50% super fine nylon / 50% super fine acrylic; 100 grams / 150 yards): 21 (12) skeins #5703 Barley

Needles
One 36" (90 cm) long or longer circular (circ) needle size US 10½ (6.5 mm)
Change needle size if necessary to obtain correct gauge.

Gauge
16 sts and 19 rows = 4" (10 cm) in Basketweave Stitch

Stitch Pattern
BASKETWEAVE STITCH (multiple of 8 sts + 4; 14-row repeat)
Rows 1 (RS), 3, 5, 8, 10, and 12: *K4, p4; repeat from * to last 4 sts, k4.
Rows 2, 4, 9, and 11: *P4, k4; repeat from * to last 4 sts, p4.
Rows 6, 7, 13, and 14: Knit.
Repeat Rows 1-14 for Basketweave Stitch.

Afghan
CO 252 (180) sts. Begin Basketweave st; work even until piece measures approximately 72 (55)" from the beginning, ending with either Row 5 or 12 of Basketweave st. BO all sts.

Finishing
Block lightly (see Special Techniques, page 158).

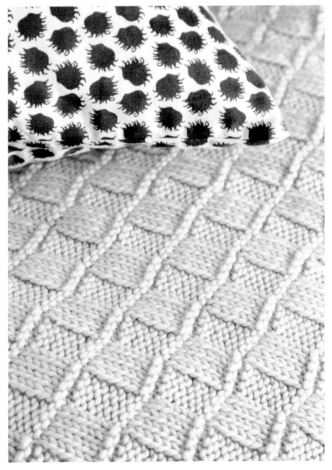

Garter Stripes

Composed of three separate garter-stitch strips that are sewn together at the end, this afghan is the ultimate in easy knitting. Each panel is worked in two colors, with the nonworking yarn carried along the side, leaving very few loose ends to weave in later. A doubled-yarn overcast-stitch border lends a refined finish.

Finished Measurements

66" wide x 60" long

Yarn

Berroco Comfort Chunky (50% super fine nylon / 50% super fine acrylic; 100 grams / 150 yards): 7 skeins each #5734 Liquorice (A) and #5760 Beet Root (C); 6 skeins #5713 Dusk (B)

Needles

One pair straight needles size US 10½ (6.5 mm)
Change needle size if necessary to obtain correct gauge.

Gauge

14 sts and 24 rows = 4" (10 cm) in Garter stitch (knit every row)

Afghan

STRIP A
Using A, CO 73 sts.
Rows 1 and 2: Knit.
Rows 3 and 4: Change to B. Knit.
Repeat Rows 1-4 until Strip measures 60" from the beginning.
BO all sts.

STRIP B
Using C, CO 73 sts.
Rows 1 and 2: Knit.
Rows 3 and 4: Change to B. Knit.
Repeat Rows 1-4 until Strip measures 60" from the beginning.
BO all sts.

STRIP C
Using C, CO 73 sts.
Rows 1 and 2: Knit.
Rows 3 and 4: Change to A. Knit.
Repeat Rows 1-4 until Strip measures 60" from the beginning.
BO all sts.

Finishing

Sew Strips A, B, and C together.
Using 2 strands of A held together, work Overcast Stitch (see Special Techniques, page 157) evenly around entire afghan.
Block lightly (see Special Techniques, page 158).

Westchester
Winter

Silhouetted trees with bare winter branches are mirrored and then reflected downward, forming an abstract pattern of dark and light on this pictorial afghan. The pattern gets its name from the Sawmill River Parkway in Westchester, New York, which is lined with large and looming trees that lend a mysterious air at dusk during winter. A thoughtful combination of intarsia and stranded knitting works best when tackling this art piece.

Finished Measurements
34" wide x 46" long

Yarn
Berroco Comfort (50% super fine nylon / 50% super fine acrylic; 100 grams / 210 yards): 5 skeins #9703 Barley (A); 4 skeins #9741 Bitter Sweet (B)

Needles
One 36" (90 cm) long or longer circular (circ) needle size US 8 (5 mm)
Change needle size if necessary to obtain correct gauge.

Notions
Crochet hook size US H/8 (5 mm)

Gauge
20 sts and 24 rows = 4" (10 cm) over Westchester Winter Chart

Afghan
Using A, CO 160 sts. Begin pattern from Westchester Winter Chart; work sts 1-80 once, then reverse pattern by working sts 80-1 once. Work even until Row 132 is complete, then reverse pattern by working Rows 132-1. BO all sts.

Finishing
With RS facing, using crochet hook and B, work 2 rnds of dc around entire afghan, working 3 dc in each corner.
Block lightly (see Special Techniques, page 158).

132
130
128
126
124
122
120
118
116
114
112
110
108
106
104
102
100
98
96
94
92
90
88
86
84
82
80
78
76
74
72
70
68
66
64
62
60
58
56
54
52
50
48
46
44
42
40
38
36
34
32
30
28
26
24
22
20
18
16
14
12
10
8
6
4
2

131
129
127
125
123
121
119
117
115
113
111
109
107
105
103
101
99
97
95
93
91
89
87
85
83
81
79
77
75
73
71
69
67
65
63
61
59
57
55
53
51
49
47
45
43
41
39
37
35
33
31
29
27
25
23
21
19
17
15
13
11
9
7
5
3
1

79 77 75 73 71 69 67 65 63 61 59 57 55 53 51 49 47 45 43 41 39 37 35 33 31 29 27 25 23 21 19 17 15 13 11 9 7 5 3 1

KEY

Knit on RS, purl on WS.

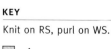

A

B

Crazy

Patchwork crazy quilts were all the rage in the late 1880s, inspired by a trend toward exoticism combined with nostalgia for the home-made look that preceded the Industrial Revolution. These quilts were dubbed "crazy" because of their unplanned look, though they were usually plotted very meticulously. Our crocheted version pays homage to the look of the originals, using colors authentic to that era as well as a touch of decorative embroidery.

Finished Measurements

41" wide x 61" long

Yarn

Berroco Comfort (50% super fine nylon / 50% super fine acrylic; 100 grams / 210 yards): 3 skeins each #9747 Cadet (A), #9762 Spruce (C), #9717 Raspberry Coulis (D), and #9780 Dried Plum (E); 2 skeins #9724 Pumpkin (B)
Berroco Comfort Chunky (50% super fine nylon / 50% super fine acrylic; 100 grams / 150 yards): 1 skein #5703 Barley (F)

Crochet Hook

Crochet hook size US I/9 (5.5 mm)
Change hook size if necessary to obtain correct gauge.

Gauge

14 sts and 17 rows = 4" (10 cm) in Single Crochet (sc)

Stitch Pattern

SINGLE CROCHET (sc) (any number of sts + 1 ch; 1-row repeat)
Set-Up Row: Sc in 2nd ch from hook and in each ch across, turn.
All Rows: Ch 1, sc in each sc across, turn.

Special Stitches

Decrease at beginning of row: Ch1, sc in first sc, skip next sc, work to end of row.
Decrease at end of row: Work in pattern to last 2 sc, skip 1 sc, sc in last st.

Afghan

SQUARE 1 (make 3)
Square measures approximately 20" x 20"

Section A: Using A, ch 39. Begin Single Crochet (sc); work even for 4".
Next Row (RS): Decrease 1 st at end of row.
Next Row: Decrease 1 st at beginning of row.
Repeat last 2 rows until 2 sts remain.
Next Row: Decrease 2 sts together. Fasten off.

Section B: With RS facing, using B, work 42 sc along right-hand edge of Section A. Work even for 1 row.
Next Row: Working in back loop only of each sc, work 1 decrease at end of row.
Next Row: Working through both loops, work even.
Repeat last 2 rows until 6 sts remain. Fasten off.

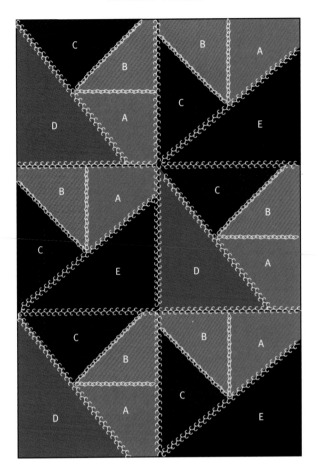

KEY

 ZigZag Chain St   Feather St

Section C: With RS facing, using C, work 49 sc along right-hand edge of Section B.
*Next Row (WS): Decrease 1 st at end of row.
Next Row: Decrease 1 st at beginning of row.
Repeat last 2 rows twice. Work even for 1 row.
Next Row (RS): Decrease 1 st at beginning of row.
Next Row: Decrease 1 st at end of row.
Repeat last 2 rows twice. Work even for 1 row.
Repeat from * until 3 sts remain. Decrease 3 sc together.
Fasten off.

Section D: With RS facing, using D, work 90 sc across left-hand edge of Section C and top of Section A.
*Next Row (WS): Decrease 1 st at beginning and end of row.
Next Row: Working through back loops only of sc, decrease 1 st at beginning and end of row.
Next Row: Working through both loops, decrease 1 st at beginning and end of row.
Next Row: Work even.
Repeat from * until 4 sts remain.
Next Row: Decrease 2 st together twice.
Next Row: Decrease 2 sts together. Fasten off.

SQUARE 2 (make 3)
Work same as for Square 1 for Sections A, B, and C.
Section E: Using E, work same as for Section D of Square 1.

Finishing

Arrange Squares together following Assembly Diagram.
Border: With RS facing, using E, work sc around entire afghan, working (sc, ch 1, sc) in each corner, join with sl st in first sc, ch 1, work another rnd of sc around afghan, working 3 sc in ch-1 sp at each corner. Join with a sl st and fasten off.
Embroidery: Using F, work embroidery following Assembly Diagram.
Block lightly (see Special Techniques, page 158).

ZIGZAG CHAIN ST

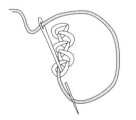

FEATHER ST

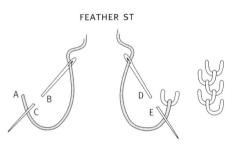

Textured
Knots

Basic two-over-two cables combine to form a lattice of intricate knots, diagonal arcs, and highly twisted ropes on this classic, textured afghan. The top and bottom of the afghan are ribbed, and the side edges are worked in garter stitch, which means there's no finishing to do once you have bound off except for weaving in a few ends and lightly blocking.

Finished Measurements

52" wide x 62" long

Yarn

Berroco Comfort (50% super fine nylon / 50% super fine acrylic; 100 grams / 210 yards): 17 skeins #9756 Copen Blue

Needles

One 36" (90 cm) long or longer circular (circ) needle size US 6 (4 mm)
One 36" (90 cm) long or longer circular needle size US 8 (5 mm)
Change needle size if necessary to obtain correct gauge.

Notions

Cable needle (cn); stitch markers

Gauge

24 sts and 22 rows = 4" (10 cm) in pattern from Knot Chart, using larger needles

Afghan

Using smaller needle, CO 308 sts.

Set-Up Row (RS): Work 5 sts in Garter st (knit every row), place marker (pm), work Section A of Knot Chart once, pm work Section B to last 19 sts, pm, work Section C once, pm, work in Garter st to end. Keeping first and last 5 sts in Garter st, repeat Rows 1 and 2 of Chart for 2", ending with a WS row. Change to larger needle and work even until entire Chart is complete. Repeat Rows 1-32 of Chart until piece measures approximately 60" from the beginning, ending with Row 32. Change to smaller needles. Repeat Rows 1 and 2 of Chart for 2". BO all sts.

Finishing

Block lightly (see Special Techniques, page 158).

KNOT CHART

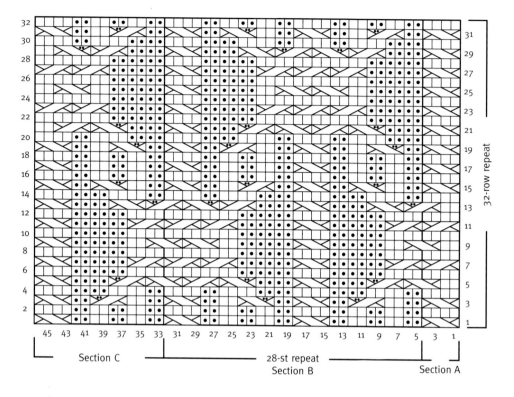

32-row repeat

45 43 41 39 37 35 33 31 29 27 25 23 21 19 17 15 13 11 9 7 5 3 1

Section C

28-st repeat
Section B

Section A

KEY

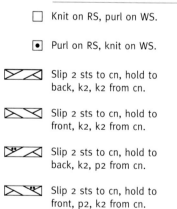

☐ Knit on RS, purl on WS.

⊡ Purl on RS, knit on WS.

◰ Slip 2 sts to cn, hold to back, k2, k2 from cn.

◱ Slip 2 sts to cn, hold to front, k2, k2 from cn.

◲ Slip 2 sts to cn, hold to back, k2, p2 from cn.

◳ Slip 2 sts to cn, hold to front, p2, k2 from cn.

While houndstooth is a classic pattern that originated in the Scottish lowlands, the design in our knitted version is enlarged so that it feels bolder and more modern. This elegant throw could easily fit into a mid-century modern living room or a masculine reading room. Brighten the color scheme and it could even look like pop art.

Finished Measurements

49" wide x 60" long

Yarn

Berroco Comfort Chunky (50% super fine nylon / 50% super fine acrylic; 100 grams / 150 yards): 8 skeins #5720 Hummus (MC); 6 skeins #5734 Liquorice (A)

Needles

One 36" (90 cm) long or longer circular (circ) needle size US 10½ (6.5 mm)
One 36" (90 cm) long or longer circular needle size US 8 (5 mm)
Change needle size if necessary to obtain correct gauge.

Gauge

16 sts and 16 rows = 4" (10 cm) in Houndstooth Pattern from Chart, using larger needles

Throw

Using larger needle and MC, CO 184 sts. Begin Houndstooth Pattern from Chart; work even until piece measures 57" from the beginning, ending with Row 8 of Chart. Change to MC. BO all sts.

Finishing

Edging: With RS facing, using smaller needle and MC, pick up and knit 240 sts evenly spaced along side edge. Begin Garter st (knit every row); work even for 1½". BO all sts knitwise. Repeat for opposite side edge. With RS facing, using smaller needle and MC, pick up and knit 195 sts evenly spaced along CO edge, including side edges. Begin Garter st; work even for 1½". BO all sts knitwise. Repeat for BO edge.
Block lightly (see Special Techniques, page 158).

HOUNDSTOOTH PATTERN

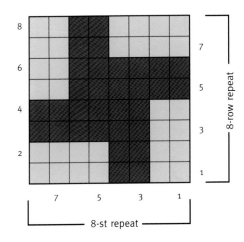

8-row repeat

8-st repeat

KEY

Knit on RS, purl on WS.

 MC

A

Irish Floral

The flowers and leaves of this throw are plucked directly from traditional Irish crochet. The thread used for Irish crochet is typically a very fine ecru or white, but the richly colored hues we chose here are feminine and moody and make the shapes stand out vibrantly from the background. The motifs are also worked at a larger gauge than is typical in Irish crochet, creating an appliquéd effect. When the shapes are completed, they are joined using an improvised chain mesh. Improvising is both challenging and fun, and lends the afghan a loose, organic shape.

Finished Measurements
43" square

Yarn
Berroco Comfort (50% super fine nylon / 50% super fine acrylic; 100 grams / 210 yards): 5 skeins #9734 Liquorice (A); 4 skeins #9721 Sprig (B); 3 skeins each #9717 Raspberry Coulis (C) and #9780 Dried Plum (D); 2 skeins each #9739 Grape Jelly (E) and #9754 Rabe (F)

Crochet Hook
Crochet hook size US G/6 (4 mm)
Change hook size if necessary to obtain correct gauge.

Gauge
16 sc and 20 rows = 4" (10 cm) in Single Crochet (sc)

Afghan
CROCHET FLOWERS
Small Flower (make 25)
Using E, ch 10, sl st to form ring. Ch 1, work 14 sc into ring, end sl st in first sc.
Rnd 1: *Sl st in first sc, ch 6, sl st in next sc. Do not turn. Bring working yarn under ch-6, work 8 sc into ch-6 loop, begin at the beginning of the ch; repeat from * 6 times. Fasten off.

Medium Flower (make 24)
Using D, ch 12, sl st to form ring. Ch 1, work 18 sc into ring, end sl st in first sc.
Rnd 1: *Sl st in first sc, ch 7, sl st in next sc. Do not turn. Bring working yarn under ch-7, work 9 sc into ch-7 loop, begin at the beginning of the ch; repeat from * 8 times. Fasten off.

Large Flower (make 17)
Using C, ch 16, sl st to form ring. Ch 1, work 20 sc into ring, end sl st in first sc.

Rnd 1: *Sl st in first sc, ch 20, sl st in next sc. Do not turn. Bring working yarn under ch-20, work 22 sc into ch-20 loop, begin at the beginning of the ch; repeat from * 9 times. Fasten off.

SMALL LEAF (make 11)
Stem: Using F, ch 27, sc in 2nd ch from hook and in each ch across to last ch, work 3 sc in last ch, continue to work 1 sc in the bottom of each ch, end 2 in last st, sl st to beg sc. Break yarn.
Leaf: With WS of Stem facing, using B, beg in 12th sc from end, work 16 sc, 3 sc in point (center st of previous 3 sc), 16 sc. Turn. *Sl st in first sc, sc in each sc to center of point, work 3 sc in point, sc to within 2 sc. Turn. Repeat from * 4 times. Fasten off.

LARGE LEAF (make 8)
Stem: Using F, ch 41. Sc in 2nd ch from hook and in each ch across to last ch. Work 3 sc in last ch, continue to work 1 sc in the bottom of each ch, end 2 sc in last st, sl st to first sc. Break yarn.
Leaf: With WS of Stem facing, using B, beg in 17th sc from end, work 25 sc, 3 sc in point (center st of previous 3 sc), work 25 sc. Turn. *Sl st in first sc, sc in each sc to center point, work 3 sc in point, sc to within last 2 sc. Turn. Repeat from * 4 times. Fasten off.

Finishing
Edging (for each Flower and Leaf): Using A, sl st in st along edge of piece, *ch 3, sl st into another st; repeat from * around.
Joining: Arrange pieces randomly (or see photo), into a rough 43" Square. Join all pieces together as follows: Using A, sl st in st along edge of piece, *ch 3 or 4, sl st into adjacent piece, ch 3 or 4, sl st into first piece; repeat from * until all pieces are joined.
Block lightly (see Special Techniques, page 158).

Mistletoe

This afghan begins with a base of simple single crochet squares that are embellished with fancifully embroidered flowers, winterberries, and mistletoe and then crocheted together. Precision is not required. In fact, the more relaxed and folksy the embellishment, the better.

Finished Measurements
40" wide x 68" long

Yarn
Berroco Comfort DK (50% super fine nylon / 50% super fine acrylic; 50 grams / 178 yards): 6 skeins each #2703 Barley (A) and #2730 Teaberry (E); 4 skeins each #2744 Teal (C) and #2723 Rosebud (D); 3 skeins #2762 Spruce (B); 2 skeins #2760 Beet Root (F)

Crochet Hook
Crochet hook size US H/8 (5 mm)
Change hook size if necessary to obtain correct gauge.

Gauge
14 sts and 18 rows = 4" (10 cm) in Single Crochet (sc)

ASSEMBLY DIAGRAM

A	D	C	D	C	D	C	A
B	D	C	D	C	D	C	B
B	B	A	C	C	B	A	B
C	D	D	A	B	D	D	B
C	D	B	B	B	B	D	A
C	A	A	C	C	A	A	A
A	A	A	C	C	A	A	C
A	D	B	B	B	B	D	C
B	D	D	B	A	D	D	C
B	A	B	C	C	A	B	B
B	C	D	C	D	C	D	B
C	A	D	A	D	A	D	A

Throw

MOTIF A (make 24)
Using A, ch 17. Begin Single Crochet (sc) st; work for 18 rows. Fasten off.
Border: Change to B. Join with sl st at corner, *ch 5, sc in 3rd sc; repeat from * around the motif, working 6 ch-5 loops on each side. Work embroidery following Chart for Motif A.

MOTIF B (make 24)
Using C, ch 17. Begin Single Crochet st; *work 2 rows C, then 2 rows A; repeat from * for 18 rows. Fasten off. Work Border as for Motif A. Work embroidery following Chart for Motif B.

MOTIF C (make 24)
Using D, work as for Motif A. Work Border as for Motif A. Work embroidery following Chart for Motif C.

MOTIF D (make 24)
Using E, work as for Motif A. Work Border as for Motif A. Work embroidery following Chart for Motif D.

Finishing
Arrange Motifs following Assembly Diagram. Using C, join with sl st at one corner and join all Motifs as follows: *Ch 2, 1 sc in ch-5 space of first Motif, ch 2, 1 sc in ch-5 space of adjacent Motif, repeat from * across.
Block lightly (see Special Techniques, page 158).

KEY

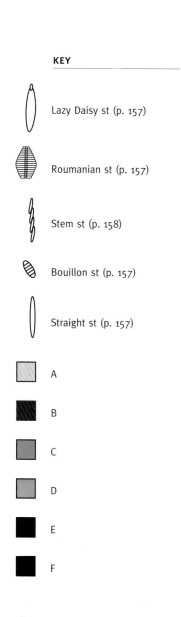

Lazy Daisy st (p. 157)

Roumanian st (p. 157)

Stem st (p. 158)

Bouillon st (p. 157)

Straight st (p. 157)

A

B

C

D

E

F

MOTIF A

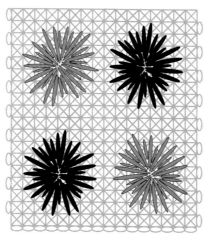

MOTIF B

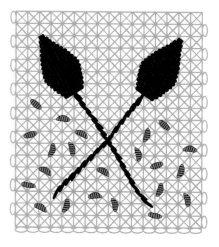

MOTIF C

MOTIF D

Little Waves

For this baby blanket, softly undulating waves ripple in all directions in a soothing palette of pastels and neutrals. Squares are made with easy crochet stitches in two different stripe sequences and are sewn together in a basketweave arrangement.

Finished Measurements
40" Square

Yarn
Berroco Comfort (50% super fine nylon / 50% super fine acrylic; 100 grams / 210 yards): 3 skeins #9701 Ivory (A); 2 skeins each #9708 Grape Fuzz (B), #9714 Robins Egg (D), and #9707 Boy Blue (E); 1 skein #9703 Barley (C)

Crochet Hook
Crochet hook size US H/8 (5 mm)
Change hook size if necessary to obtain correct gauge.

Gauge
14 sts and 15 rows = 4" (10 cm) in Single Crochet (sc)

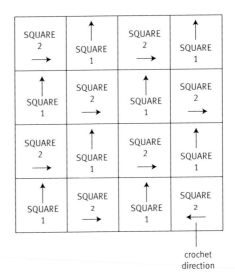

crochet
direction

Afghan

SQUARE 1 (make 8)

Using A, ch 36. Begin Single Crochet (sc); work even for 1 row–35 sts.

Rows 1-13: Continuing in sc, change colors as follows: 3 rows A, 1 row B, 1 row C, 1 row D, 4 rows A, 1 row B, 1 row C, then 1 row B.

Row 14: Change to D. Ch 3 (counts as 1 dc), skip first sc, dc in each of the next 2 sc, *hdc in next sc, sc in each of the next 3 sc, hdc in next sc, dc in each of the next 3 sc; repeat from * across, turn.

Rows 15-17: Ch 3 (counts as 1 dc), skip first dc, dc in each of the next 2 dc, *hdc in next hdc, sc in each of the next 3 sc, hdc in next hdc, dc in each of the next 3 dc; repeat from * across, turn.

Row 18: Change to B. Ch 1, sc in each st across, turn.

Row 19: Change to C. Work in sc.

Row 20: Change to B. Work in sc.

Row 21: Change to E. Ch 1, sc in each of the next 3 sc, *hdc in next sc, dc in each of the next 3 sc, hdc in next sc, sc in each of the next 3 sc; repeat from * across, turn.

Row 22-24: Change to E. Ch 1, sc in each of the next 3 sc, *hdc in next hdc, dc in each of the next 3 dc, hdc in next hdc, sc in each of the next 3 sc; repeat from * across, turn.

Row 25: Change to B. Ch 1, sc in each st across, turn.

Rows 26-38: Continuing in sc, change colors as follows: 1 row C, 1 row B, 4 rows A, 1 row E, 1 row C, 1 row B, then 4 rows A. Fasten off.

SQUARE 2 (make 8)

Using A, ch 36. Begin Single Crochet (sc); work even for 1 row–35 sts.

Rows 1-4: Continuing in sc, change colors as follows: 1 row B, 1 row C, 1 row B, then 1 row A.

Row 5: Change to E. Ch 3 (counts as 1 dc), skip first sc, dc in each of the next 2 sc, *hdc in next sc, sc in each of the next 3 sc, hdc in next sc, dc in each of the next 3 sc; repeat from * across, turn.

Rows 6-8: Ch 3 (counts as 1 dc), skip first dc, dc in each of the next 2 dc, *hdc in next hdc, sc in each of the next 3 sc, hdc in next hdc, dc in each of the next 3 dc; repeat from * across, turn.

Row 9: Change to A. Ch 1, sc in each st across, turn.

Rows 10-13: Repeat Rows 1-4.

Row 14: Change to D. Ch 1, sc in each of the next 3 sc, *hdc in next sc, dc in each of the next 3 sc, hdc in next sc, sc in each of the next 3 sc; repeat from * across, turn.

Row 15-17: Ch 1, sc in each of the next 3 sc, *hdc in next hdc, dc in each of the next 3 dc, hdc in next hdc, sc in each of the next 3 sc; repeat from * across, turn.

Row 18: Change to A. Ch 1, sc in each st across, turn.

Rows 19-38: Repeat Rows 1-20.

Finishing

Sew Squares together following Assembly Diagram.

Edging: With RS facing, using A, sl st in any st at edge of throw, work in sc around entire outer edge of throw, working 3 sc in each corner, join with a sl st in first sc. Working in sc, work 1 rnd B, 1 rnd C, then 1 rnd B. Fasten off.

Block lightly (see Special Techniques, page 158).

Meditate

For this easy afghan, two soothing colors and two basic stitches, single crochet and chain, create a visual rhythm that looks complex but is actually quite simple. The alternating dominance of light and dark—achieved by working more rows of one shade than the other—forms a gradation that almost appears dip-dyed.

Finished Measurements
45" wide x 60" long

Yarn
Berroco Comfort (50% super fine nylon / 50% super fine acrylic; 100 grams / 210 yards): 7 skeins each #9757 Lillet (A) and #9728 Raspberry Sorbet (B)

Crochet Hook
Crochet hook size US H/8 (5 mm)
Change hook size if necessary to obtain correct gauge.

Gauge
18 sts and 17 rows = 4" (10 cm) in Single Crochet Mesh

Stitch Patterns
SINGLE CROCHET MESH (multiple of 4 sts + 2; 2-row repeat)
Set-Up Row: Sc in 2nd ch from hook, *ch 1, skip 1 ch, sc in next ch; repeat from * to end, turn.
Row 1: Ch 2 (counts as a sc and ch 1 sp), *sc in ch-1 sp, ch 1; repeat from * to last st, sc in last ch, turn.
Row 2: Ch 1, sc in 1st ch 1 sp, *ch 1, sc in next ch 1 sp; repeat from * to end.
Repeat Rows 1 and 2 for Single Crochet Mesh.

STRIPE SEQUENCE
Work *[1 row B, 1 row A] 3 times, 1 row B, [2 rows A, 1 row B] 3 times, [4 rows A, 1 row B] twice, [1 row A, 2 rows B] 4 times, 5 rows B, [1 row A, 1 row B] 3 times, then 2 rows A; repeat from * for Stripe Sequence.

Throw
Using A, ch 210. Begin Single Crochet Mesh; work Set-Up Row. Continuing in Single Crochet Mesh, begin Stripe Sequence; work even until piece measures 60" from the beginning. Fasten off.

Finishing
Block lightly (see Special Techniques, page 158).

Mindful

Dramatic increases and decreases give this afghan its mazelike appearance. It is composed of a series of strips, each one consisting of large and small rectangles, that are edged in a contrasting color and then crocheted to one another like puzzle pieces. The result is a refined and complex-looking design that is actually fairly simple to achieve.

Finished Measurements

45" wide x 60" long

Yarn

Berroco Comfort (50% super fine nylon / 50% super fine acrylic; 100 grams / 210 yards): 15 skeins #9720 Hummus (MC); 4 skeins #9741 Bitter Sweet (A)

Crochet Hook

Crochet hook size US H/8 (5 mm)
Change hook size if necessary to obtain correct gauge.

Gauge

14 sts and 18 rows = 4" (10 cm) in Single Crochet (sc)

Afghan

STRIP 1 (make 8)
Using MC, ch 21. *Begin sc; work even until piece measures 8½" from the beginning, turn.
Next Row: Sl st across 8 sc, ch 1, sc in each of the next 4 sc, turn. Work even in sc on 4 sts for 9½", turn.
Next Row: Ch 9, sc in 2nd ch from hook and in each ch and sc across–12 sc, turn.
Next Row: Ch 9, sc in 2nd ch from hook and in each ch and sc across–20 sc, turn. Repeat from * once, then work even in sc for 8½". Fasten off.

STRIP 2 (make 7)
Using MC, ch 5. *Begin sc; work even until piece measures 9½" from the beginning, turn.
Next Row: Ch 9, sc in 2nd ch from hook and in each ch and sc across–12 sc, turn.
Next Row: Ch 9, sc in 2nd ch from hook and in each ch and sc across–20 sc, turn. Work even in sc for 8½", turn.
Next Row: Sl st across 8 sc, ch 1, sc in each of the next 4 sc, turn. Repeat from * once, then work even on 4 sc for 9½".
Fasten off.

FILLER STRIP (make 4)
Using MC, ch 8. Begin sc; work until piece measures 8½" from the beginning. Fasten off.

Finishing

Strip Edging: Using A, work in sc around outside edge of every Strip, working corners as follows: Work 3 scs in each outer corner. In each inner corner, pull up a loop before corner, in corner, then after corner, yo and pull through all 4 loops on hook (decreasing 2 scs). Join with a sl st in beg sc. Fasten off. Sew Strips 1 and 2 together, interlocking the rectangles. Sew the 4 filler Strips into open rectangle spaces at sides.
Outer Edging: With RS facing, using A, work sc around entire throw, working 3 sc in each corner. Join with a sl st in first sc. Fasten off.
Block lightly (see Special Techniques, page 158).

Autumn Haze

This striped afghan is a celebration of the New England countryside in autumn. The yellows and oranges of sugar maples and the incredible red of viburnum are tempered by the soft green of spruce needles and the perennial greens of pine. Worked in one piece with minimal finishing, it will keep you warm as you work on it.

Finished Measurements
45" wide x 60" long

Yarn
Berroco Comfort (50% super fine nylon / 50% super fine acrylic; 100 grams / 210 yards): 3 skeins each #9781 Olive (A) and #9721 Sprig (B); 2 skeins each #9745 Filbert (C), #9743 Goldenrod (D), #9754 Rabe (E), #9724 Pumpkin (F), and #9760 Beet Root (G)

Needles
One 36" (90 cm) long or longer circular (circ) needle size US 8 (5 mm)
Change needle size if necessary to obtain correct gauge.

Gauge
20 sts and 27 rows = 4" (10 cm) in Stockinette st (St st)

Afghan
Using A, CO 215 sts.

Rows 1 (RS)-6: Knit.

Rows 7 and 8: Change to B. Knit.

Row 9: K1, *slip 1 wyib, k3; repeat from * to last 2 sts, slip 1 wyib, k1.

Row 10: Change to C. P3, *slip 1 wyif, p3; repeat from * to end.

Row 11: Change to D. K1, *slip 1 wyib, k3; repeat from * to last 2 sts, slip 1 wyib, k1.

Row 12: Change to A. P3, *slip 1 wyif, p3; repeat from * to end.

Row 13: Change to C. K1, *slip 1 wyib, k3; repeat from * to last 2 sts, slip 1 wyib, k1.

Row 14: Change to B. P3, *slip 1 wyif, p3; repeat from * to end.

Row 15: Change to A. K1, *slip 1 wyib, k3; repeat from * to last 2 sts, slip 1 wyib, k1.

Row 16: Change to D. P3, *slip 1 wyif, p3; repeat from * to end.

Rows 17-32: Repeat Rows 9-16.

Rows 33-36: Change to B. Knit.

Row 37: Change to E. Knit.

Row 38: Change to A. Knit.

Rows 39-48: Change to B. Work in St st.

Rows 49 and 50: Change to C. Knit.

Rows 51-53: Change to G. Knit.

Row 54: Change to F. Knit.

Row 55: K1, *p1, k1; repeat from * to end.

Row 56: Purl.

Row 57: P1, *k1, p1; repeat from * to end.

Row 58: Purl.

Rows 59-62: Repeat Rows 55-58.

Rows 63 and 64: Change to E. Knit.

Rows 65 and 66: Change to B. Knit.

Row 67: Change to A. Knit.

Row 68: Change to D. Knit.

Rows 69-76: Work in St st.

Rows 77-79: Change to C. Knit.

Rows 80-82: Change to A. Knit.

Row 83: Change to G. K1, *slip 1 wyib, k3; repeat from * to last 2 sts, slip 1 wyib, k1.

Row 84: Change to F. P3, *slip 1 wyif, p3; repeat from * to end.

Row 85: Change to D. K1, *slip 1 wyib, k3; repeat from * to last 2 sts, slip 1 wyib, k1.

Row 86: Change to G. P3, *slip 1 wyif, p3; repeat from * to end.

Row 87: Change to A. K1, *slip 1 wyib, k3; repeat from * to last 2 sts, slip 1 wyib, k1.

Row 88: Change to D. P3, *slip 1 wyif, p3; repeat from * to end.

Row 89: Change to F. K1, *slip 1 wyib, k3; repeat from * to last 2 sts, slip 1 wyib, k1.

Row 90: Change to A. P3, *slip 1 wyif, p3; repeat from * to end.

Rows 91-106: Repeat Rows 83-90.

Rows 107-110: Change to B. Knit.

Rows 111 and 112: Change to G. Knit.

Row 113: Change to E. K1, *p1, k1; repeat from * to end.

Row 114: Purl.

Row 115: P1, *k1, p1; repeat from * to end.

Row 116: Purl.

Rows 117-124: Repeat Rows 113-116.

Rows 125 and 126: Change to C. Knit.

Rows 127-129: Change to D. Knit.

Row 130: Change to F. Knit.

Rows 131-138: Work in St st.

Rows 139 and 140: Change to E. Knit.

Rows 141-143: Change to B. Knit.

Row 144: Change to G. Knit.

Row 145: K1, *p1, k1; repeat from * to end.

Row 146: Purl.

Row 147: P1, *k1, p1; repeat from * to end.

Row 148: Purl.

Rows 149-152: Repeat Rows 145-148.

Rows 153-456: Repeat Rows 1-152 twice.

Rows 457 and 458: Change to B. Knit.

Rows 459-464: Change to A. Knit.

BO all sts.

Finishing

Side Edging: With RS facing, using circ needle and B, pick up and knit 310 sts evenly spaced along side edge. Knit 1 row. Change to A. Knit 6 rows. BO all sts. Repeat for second side edge. Block lightly (see Special Techniques, page 158).

Stella

In this crocheted afghan, easy "granny" triangles are edged with a contrasting color in a meshlike pattern to create hexagons, which are then embellished with bright flowers. We attached only the centers of the flowers to the hexagons so the petals would curl up like real blossoms. For a more structured, geometric look, you could leave off the flowers.

Finished Measurements
48" wide x 60" long

Yarn
Berroco Comfort (50% super fine nylon / 50% super fine acrylic; 100 grams / 210 yards): 14 skeins #9745 Filbert (A); 7 skeins #9754 Rabe (B); 1 skein each #9722 Purple (C), #9721 Sprig (D), and #9742 Pimpernel (E)

Crochet Hook
Crochet hook size US H/8 (5 mm)
Change hook size if necessary to obtain correct gauge.

Gauge
16 sts and 10 rows = 4" (10 cm) in Double Crochet (dc)

ASSEMBLY DIAGRAM

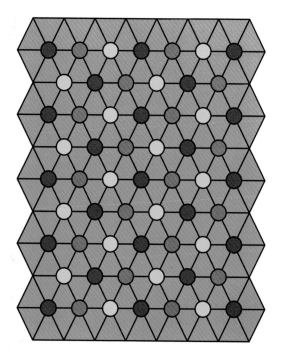

KEY

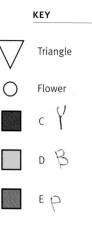

▽ Triangle

○ Flower

■ C

□ D

▨ E

Afghan

TRIANGLE MOTIF (make 150)
Using A, ch 6, join with a sl st to form a ring.
Rnd 1: Ch 8 (counts as 1 dc and ch-5), *5 dc in ring, ch 5; repeat from * once, 4 dc in ring, join with a sl st in 3rd ch of ch-8.
Rnds 2-4: Sl st in each of the next 2 ch, ch 8 (counts as 1 dc and ch-5), 2 dc in same ch-5 sp, *dc in each dc to next ch-5 sp, (2 dc, ch 5, 2 dc) in ch-5 sp; repeat from * once, dc in each dc to last ch-5, dc in last ch-5 sp, join with a sl st in 3rd ch of ch-8.
Rnd 5: Change to B. Repeat Rnd 2. Fasten off.

FLOWER MOTIF
All Centers: Using B, ch 5, join with a sl st to form a ring. Ch 4 (counts as 1 hdc and ch 2), *hdc in ring, ch 2; repeat from * 4 times, join with sl st in 2nd ch of beg ch-4. Fasten off.
Petals (make 23 C, 18 each D and E)
Using C, D, or E, sl st in any center ch-2 sp. In the same sp, *1 sc, 1 dc, 3 tr, 1 dc and 1 sc (petal made), repeat from * in each ch-2 sp around, join with a sl st in first sc. Fasten off.

Finishing

Sew Triangle Motifs together following Assembly Diagram. Sew Flower Motifs to Triangles following Assembly Diagram. Block lightly (see Special Techniques, page 158).

Lucy

Simple, lacy, and colorful, this lightweight throw looks fantastic adorning a sofa and can even be used as a wrap on a chilly day. The center mesh stitch is embellished with a feminine, Victorian edging, made modern with the use of a bright, contrasting color.

Finished Measurements

45" wide x 60" long

Yarn

Berroco Comfort (50% super fine nylon / 50% super fine acrylic; 100 grams / 210 yards): 6 skeins #9760 Beet Root (MC)
Berroco Comfort DK (50% super fine nylon / 50% super fine acrylic; 50 grams / 178 yards): 1 skein each #2742 Pimpernel (A) and #2721 Sprig (B)

Crochet Hooks

Crochet hook size US H/8 (5 mm)
Crochet hook size US F/5 (3.75 mm)
Change hook size if necessary to obtain correct gauge.

Gauge

9 "grids" and 14 rows = 8" (20.5 cm) in Solomon's Grid, using larger hook

Abbreviations

SK (Solomon's Knot): Pull up loop ½" - 1" long on hook (keep this consistent throughout), hold this loop steady with left hand, yo and draw through elongated st to make a 3rd strand to the same length, insert hook into side of this 3rd elongated strand, yo and draw through loop, yo and draw through 2 loops on hook.

Stitch Pattern

Solomon's Grid: (multiple of 4 sts + 3 ch; 1 row repeat)
Set-Up Row 1: 1 SK, skip 6 ch, 1 dc in next ch, *1 SK, skip 3 ch, 1 dc in next ch; repeat from * to end, turn.
Set-Up Row 2: Ch 3, *1 SK, skip first dc and 1 SK, 1 dc in dc; repeat from *, ending dc in top of ch 6, turn.
Row 3: Repeat Row 2, ending dc in top of 3 ch.
Repeat Row 3 for Solomon's Grid.

Throw

Using larger crochet hook and MC, ch 179. Begin Solomon's Grid; work even until piece measures 55" from the beginning. Fasten off.

Finishing

Coronet Trim: Using smaller crochet hook and A, attach yarn to an opening "grid" on edge of throw.
Row 1: *Work 7 sc along 2 "grids," turn, 7 ch, skip 5 sc, sc in next sc, turn, [6 sc, ch 5, 6 sc] in ch-7 sp; repeat from * around entire throw, join with a slip st. Fasten off.
Row 2: Change to B. Ch 4, *skip next 6 sc, ([1 dc, ch 3] 4 times, 1 dc) in ch-5 loop, skip 6 sc, 1 tr in next sc; repeat from * around, omitting last tr, join with sl st in top of ch-4. Fasten off. Block lightly (see Special Techniques, page 158).

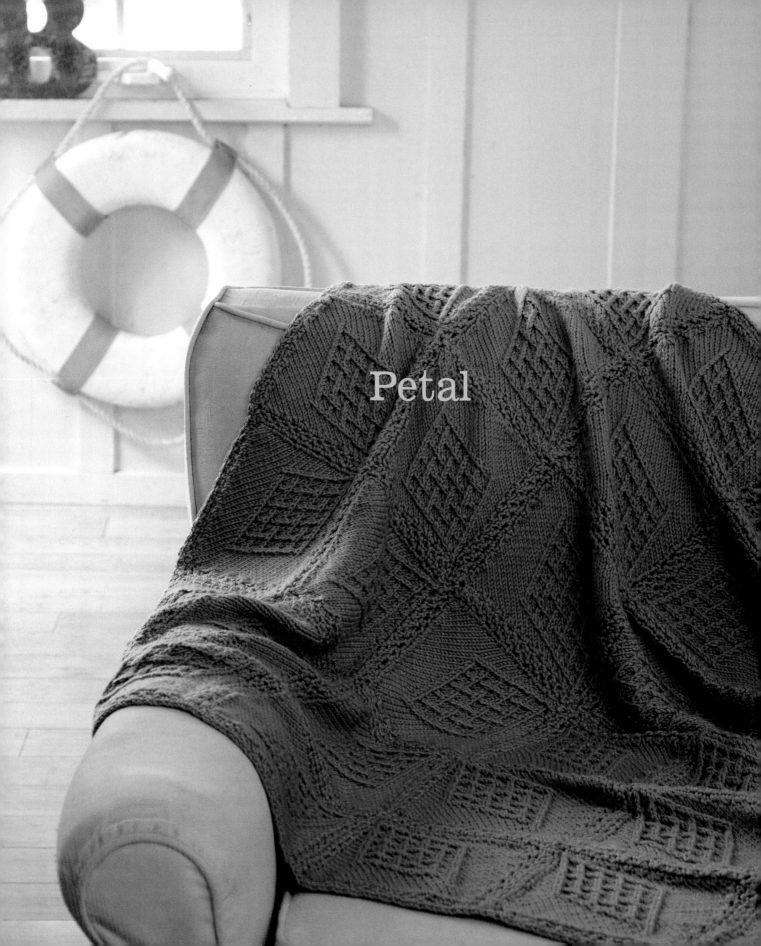

Petal

The formula for this baby blanket is simple: Repeat one square 36 times, arrange, and join. The diamonds in each square—made from twisted stitches—are joined to form a flower in the center of the blanket (see photo on page 85).

Finished Measurements

37" square

Yarn

Berroco Comfort (50% super fine nylon / 50% super fine acrylic; 100 grams / 210 yards): 7 skeins #9758 Crypto Crystalline

Needles

One pair straight needles size US 8 (5 mm)
Change needle size if necessary to obtain correct gauge.

Notions

Crochet hook size US H/8 (5 mm)

Gauge

18 sts and 24 rows = 4" (10 cm) in Stockinette stitch (St st)

Afghan

PETAL (make 36)
CO 4 sts. Begin Petal Chart; work even until Chart is completed. BO remaining 4 sts.

Edging: Using crochet hook, sl st into the beginning of one side of Petal. *(Ch 2, sc) 10 times along 1 side, (sc, ch 2, sc) in corner; repeat from * 3 times.

Finishing

Joining: Join Petals together following Assembly Diagram as follows: Beginning at corner of Petal, sl 1 into ch-2 space of first Petal, ch 1, sl 1 into ch-2 space of 2nd Petal, *ch 1, sl 1 into next ch-2 space of first Petal, ch 1, sl 1 into next ch-2 space of 2nd Petal; repeat from * along sides of Petals.

Border: Sc into any ch-2 space at edge of afghan, *ch 2, sc in next ch-2 space; repeat from * around entire afghan, working 3 sc in each corner.

Block lightly (see Special Techniques, page 158).

PETAL CHART

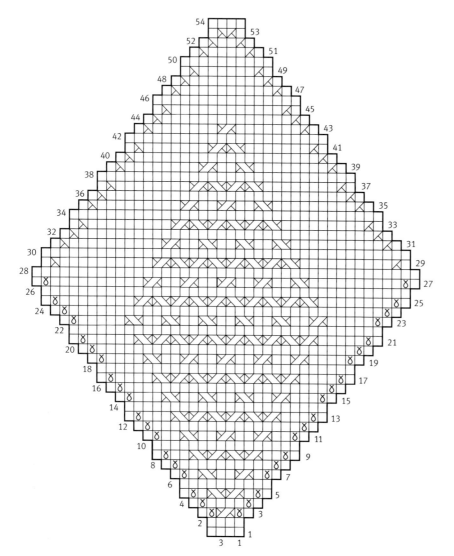

KEY

☐	Knit on RS, purl on WS.
⊠	Make 1 knitwise on RS, make 1 purlwise on WS.
⊠	K2tog on RS, p2tog on WS.
⊠	Ssk on RS, p2tog-tbl on WS.
⊠⊠	Knit into back of second st, then knit first and second sts together through back loops, slip both sts from left-hand needle together.
⊠⊠	K2tog, but do not drop sts from left-hand needle, insert right-hand needle between 2 sts just worked and knit first st again, slip both sts from left-hand needle together.

ASSEMBLY DIAGRAM

Pinwheel

An unusual technique makes this playful throw a cinch to crochet. Each square is composed of open-grid filet crochet, which is then embellished with a pinwheel of crocheted chain stitch. A contrasting color is used to connect all the pinwheels.

Finished Measurements

40" wide x 56" long

Yarn

Berroco Comfort DK (50% super fine nylon / 50% super fine acrylic; 50 grams / 178 yards): 5 skeins #2745 Filbert (A); 4 skeins #2754 Rabe (D); 3 skeins each #2721 Sprig (B) and #2722 Purple (C); 2 skeins #2730 Teaberry (E)

Crochet Hook

Crochet hook size US F/5 (3.75 mm)
Change hook size if necessary to obtain correct gauge.

Gauge

19 sts and 9 rows = 4" (10 cm) over 1 Square

Square

Ch 20.
Set-Up Row: Dc in 4th ch from hook (counts as dc, ch 1, dc), *ch 1, skip 1 ch, dc in next ch; repeat from * to end.
Rows 1-8: Ch 4 (counts as dc and ch 1), skip 1st dc, dc in next dc, *ch 1, skip 1 ch, dc in next dc; repeat from * to end. Fasten off.

Throw

SQUARE A (make 30)
Work squares using A; work Chain st Pinwheel Crochet following Diagram, using C.

SQUARE B (make 30)
Work squares using B; work Chain st Pinwheel Crochet following Diagram, using D.

SQUARE C (make 30)
Work squares using C; work Chain st Pinwheel Crochet following Diagram, using D.

SQUARE D (make 25)
Work squares using D; work Chain st Pinwheel Crochet following Diagram, using A.

SQUARE E (make 25)
Work squares using C; work Chain st Pinwheel Crochet following Diagram, using B.

Finishing

Using E and Chain st, join Squares following Assembly Diagram. Block lightly (see Special Techniques, page 158).

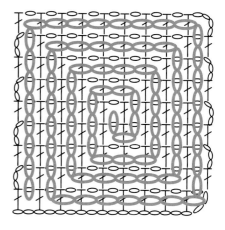

ASSEMBLY DIAGRAM

A	D	A	D	A	D	A	D	A	D
E	B	E	B	E	B	E	B	E	B
D	C	D	C	D	C	D	C	D	C
B	A	B	A	B	A	B	A	B	A
C	E	C	E	C	E	C	E	C	E
A	D	A	D	A	D	A	D	A	D
E	B	E	B	E	B	E	B	E	B
D	C	D	C	D	C	D	C	D	C
B	A	B	A	B	A	B	A	B	A
C	E	C	E	C	E	C	E	C	E
A	D	A	D	A	D	A	D	A	D
E	B	E	B	E	B	E	B	E	B
D	C	D	C	D	C	D	C	D	C
B	A	B	A	B	A	B	A	B	A

Vintage

This baby blanket is a sampler of color, texture, and cabled stitches. The colors were drawn from novelty printed fabrics of the 1950s. Some of the stripes are worked in long, thin, vertical panels, while others are worked horizontally. Fabric strips are laced through the cables, adding an unexpected whimsical touch.

Finished Measurements
30" wide x 36" long

Yarn
Berroco Comfort (50% super fine nylon / 50% super fine acrylic; 100 grams / 210 yards): 3 skeins #9703 Barley (A); 2 skeins #9781 Olive (D); 1 skein each #9749 Aunt Abbey Rose (B), #9741 Bittersweet (C), and #9721 Sprig (E)

Needles
One pair straight needles size US 8 (5 mm)
One 36" (90 cm) long or longer circular (circ) needle size US 8 (5 mm)
Change needle size if necessary to obtain correct gauge.

Notions
Crochet hook size US H/8 (5 mm); cable needle (cn);
¼ yard fabric

Gauge
20 sts and 27 rows = 4" (10 cm) in Stockinette Stitch (St st)

ASSEMBLY DIAGRAM

| A | B | A | B | A | B | A | B | A |

knitting direction

Abbreviations

C6B: Slip 3 sts to cn, hold to back, k3, k3 from cn.
C6F: Slip 3 sts to cn, hold to front, k3, k3 from cn.

Throw

STRIP A (make 5)
Using A, CO 14 sts.
Rows 1, 3, 5, and 7 (WS): K4, p6, k4.
Row 2: P4, C6B, p4.
Row 4: P4, k6, p4.
Row 6: P4, C6F, p4.
Row 8: Repeat Row 4.
Repeat Rows 1–8 until piece measures 36" from the beginning, ending with a WS row. BO all sts.

STRIP B (make 4)
With RS facing, using circ needle and B, pick up and knit 180 sts evenly along side of Strip A.
Section 1
Rows 1, 3, 5, and 7 (WS): Purl.
Rows 2 and 6: Knit.
Rows 4 and 8: *K2, yo, k2, slip yo over k2; repeat from * to end.
Row 9: Purl.

Section 2
Row 10: Change to C. *K1, p1; repeat from * to end.
Row 11: *P1, k1; repeat from * to end.
Repeat Rows 10 and 11 until Section 2 measures 1½", ending with a WS row.

Section 3
Rows 12–15: Change to D. Knit.
Row 16: *K2, yo, k2tog; repeat from * to end.
Row 17: Purl.
Rows 18–21: Knit. BO all sts.

Finishing

Sew Strips together following Assembly Diagram.
Bottom Edging: With RS facing, using circ needle and E, pick up and knit 181 sts along 1 long edge of throw.
Row 1 (WS): Purl.
Row 2: K1, *k3, p1, k6; repeat from * to end.
Row 3: P1, *p4, k1, p1, k1, p3; repeat from * to end.
Row 4: K1, *[k1, p1] 3 times, k4; repeat from * to end.
Row 5: P1, *p2, [k1, p1] 4 times; repeat from * to end.
Row 6: P1, *k1, p1, k3, [p1, k1] twice, p1; repeat from * to end.
Row 7: P1, *k1, p1, k1, p5, k1, p1; repeat from * to end.
Row 8: P1, *k7, p1, k1, p1; repeat from * to end.
Row 9: P1, *k1, p9; repeat from * to end.
Row 10: Knit.
Row 11: Change to D. Purl.
Rows 12, 14, and 16: *K3, ssk, return this st to left-hand needle, pass next st over it and slip back to right-hand needle, k3, M1-r, k1, M1-l; repeat from * to last st, k1.
Rows 13, 15, and 17: Purl.
Row 18: Repeat Row 12. BO purlwise. Repeat for Top Edge of throw.
Side Edging: With RS facing, using circ needle and E, pick up and knit 151 sts evenly spaced along side edge of throw.
Work as for Bottom Edging. Repeat on opposite edge of throw.
With RS facing, using crochet hook and D, work sc along side to cover color E. Rip four 36" strips of 2"-wide fabric. Fold strips in half lengthwise and work through eyelets of Row 16 of each piece.
Block lightly (see Special Techniques, page 158).

Floret

In this baby afghan, cables, ribs, and bobbles come together to form stylized flowers. Look carefully and you'll see that the pattern is created by repeating one basic triangle over and over. First four triangles come together to form a floret and then six florets are joined to form the blanket. The end result appears complex, but is actually derived from one simple unit.

Finished Measurements

42" square

Yarn

Berroco Comfort (50% super fine nylon / 50% super fine acrylic; 100 grams / 210 yards): 9 skeins #9744 Teal

Needles

One set of five double-pointed needles (dpn) size US 8 (5 mm)
One 16" (40 cm) circular (circ) needle size US 8 (5 mm)

Notions

Cable needle (cn); stitch markers; stitch holders

Gauge

16 sts and 24 rows = 4" (10 cm) in Stockinette stitch (St st)

Afghan

SQUARE (make 9)
Using dpns, CO 12 sts; divide sts evenly among 4 needles. Join for working in the rnd, being careful not to twist sts; place marker (pm) for beginning of rnd. Begin Chart, working increases as indicated in Chart. *Note: Change to circ needle when neccesary for number of sts on needles, placing markers between Chart repeats.* Work even until entire Chart is complete–180 sts (45 sts in each repeat). Place each 45-st section on separate st holders.

Finishing

Using Three-Needle BO, join Squares together to make one large Square.
Three-Needle BO: Place sts to be joined onto 2 same-size needles; hold pieces to be joined with RSs facing each other and needles parallel, both pointing to right. Holding both needles in your left hand, using working yarn and a 3rd needle same size or one size larger, insert 3rd needle into first st on front needle, then into first st on back needle; knit these 2 sts together; *knit next st from each needle together (2 sts on right-hand needle); pass first st over second st to BO 1 st. Repeat from * until 1 st remains on 3rd needle; cut yarn and fasten off.

Border: Slip 135 sts from 1 side of large Square onto circ needle. *K1, M1, knit to last st, M1, k1. Repeat from * until Border measures 3", ending with a RS row. BO all sts knitwise. Repeat for other sides. Sew corners.
Block lightly (see Special Techniques, page 158).

FLORET CHART

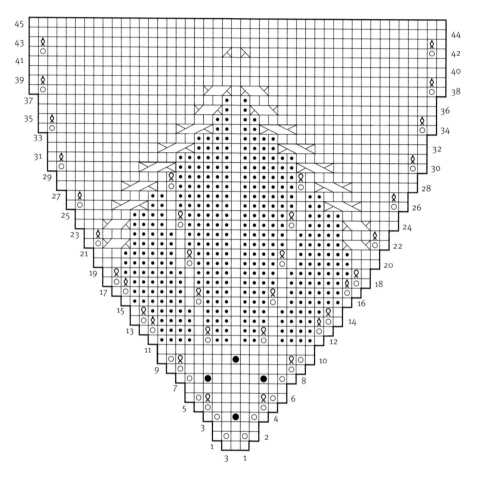

KEY

☐	Knit on RS, purl on WS.
•	Purl on RS, knit on WS.
⊙	Yo
⧄	K2tog
⧅	Ssk
●	Make Bobble: [K1-f/b] twice to increase to 4 sts, [slip 4 sts back onto left-hand needle, k4] twice, pull first, second, and third st over fourth and off needle.

℞	Knit into back loop of yo.
℞	Purl into back loop of yo.
⬔	Slip 2 sts to cn, hold to back, k2, k2 from cn.
⬔	Slip 2 sts to cn, hold to front, k2, k2 from cn.
⬔	Slip 1 st to cn, hold to back, k2, k1 from cn.
⬔	Slip 2 sts to cn, hold to front, k1, k2 from cn.

Stripe by Stripe

The browns, yellows, and blues of this baby blanket are perfect for parents who shy away from traditional baby pastels. Each piece begins with vertical stripes and is later turned on its side, with new stripe patterns added to each end. Even though only four striped patterns are repeated, each of the five strips is unique. When all of the strips are crocheted together, the results are playful and abstract.

Finished Measurements
30" wide x 36" long

Yarn
Berroco Comfort (50% super fine nylon / 50% super fine acrylic; 100 grams / 210 yards): 2 skeins each #9703 Barley (A), #9720 Hummus (B), #9726 Cornflower (C), #9712 Buttercup (D), and #9701 Ivory (E)

Crochet Hook
Crochet hook size US H/8 (5 mm)
Change hook size if necessary to obtain correct gauge.

Gauge
14 sts and 18 rows = 4" (10 cm) in Single Crochet (sc)

Blanket
STRIP 1
Block 1: Using A, ch 36. Working in Single Crochet (sc), work 4 rows A, *2 rows B, 2 rows A, 2 rows B, 4 rows A; repeat from * until piece measures 6" from the beginning. Fasten off.

Block 2: With RS facing, working along right-hand edge of Block 1, join B; work 21 sc along edge. Work 3 rows B, *2 rows E, 4 rows C, 6 rows A, 4 rows B; repeat from * until Block measures 10". Work 4 rows C, **1 row D, 1 row E, 1 row C; repeat from ** until Block measures 20". Fasten off.

Block 3: With RS facing, working along left-hand edge of Block 1, join C; work 21 sc along edge. Work 3 rows C, *1 row B, 1 row D, 1 row A, 4 rows C; repeat from * until Block measures 6". Fasten off.

STRIP 2

Block 1: Using D, ch 42. Working in Single Crochet, *work 3 rows D, 2 rows C, 2 rows B; repeat from * until Block measures 6" from the beginning. Fasten off.

Block 2: With RS facing, working along right-hand edge of Block 1, join A; work 21 sc along edge. Work 1 row A, 2 rows B, *4 rows A, 2 rows B, 2 rows A, 2 rows B; repeat from * until Block measures 12". Fasten off.

Block 3: With RS facing, working along left-hand edge of Block 1, join A; work 21 sc along edge. Work 5 rows A, *4 rows C, 2 rows E, 4 rows B, 6 rows A; repeat from * until Block measures 12". Fasten off.

STRIP 3

Block 1: Using B, ch 42. Working in Single Crochet, *work 4 rows B, 1 row E, 4 rows C, 6 rows A; repeat from * until Block measures 6" from the beginning.

Block 2: With RS facing, working along right-hand edge of Block 1, join C; work 21 sc along edge. Work 3 rows C, *1 row D, 1 row B, 1 row C; repeat from * until Block measures 12". **Work 6 rows B, 2 rows C, 4 rows D, 2 rows E; repeat from ** until Block measures 18". Fasten off.

Block 3: With RS facing, working along left-hand edge of Block 1, join D; work 21 sc along edge. Work 5 rows D, *2 rows E, 4 rows B, 2 rows C, 4 rows B, 2 rows E, 6 rows D; repeat from * until Block measures 6". Fasten off.

STRIP 4

Block 1: Using D, ch 42. Working in Single Crochet, *work 1 row D, 1 row C, 4 rows B; repeat from * until Block measures 6" from the beginning.

Block 2: With RS facing, working along right-hand edge of Block 1, join A; work 21 sc along edge. Work 5 rows A, *4 rows C, 1 row E, 4 rows B, 6 rows A; repeat from * until Block measures 12". Fasten off.

Block 3: With RS facing, working along left-hand edge of Block 1, join A; work 21 sc along edge. Work 1 row A, *2 rows B, 4 rows A, 2 rows B, 2 rows A; repeat from * until Block measures 12". Fasten off.

STRIP 5

Block 1: Using A, ch 35. Working in Single Crochet, *work 4 rows A, 2 rows B, 2 rows A, 2 rows B; repeat from * until Block measures 6" from the beginning.

Block 2: With RS facing, working along right-hand edge of Block 1, join D; work 21 sc along edge. Work 3 rows D, *1 row C, 1 row A, 1 row B, 4 rows D; repeat from * until Block measures 6". Fasten off.

Block 3: With RS facing, working along left-hand edge of Block 1, join B; work 21 sc along edge. Work 3 rows B, *2 rows E, 4 rows C, 6 rows A, 4 rows B; repeat from * until Block measures 10". Work 4 rows D, **1 row E, 1 row C, 1 row D; repeat from ** until Block measures 20". Fasten off.

Finishing

Using A, work sc around each Strip, working 3 sc in each corner. Sew Strips together in same order in which they were worked.

Edging: Using A, work sc around entire blanket, working 3 sc in each corner. Working from left to right, work 1 rnd of Reverse sc around entire blanket, working 3 Reverse sc in each corner. Fasten off.

Block lightly (see Special Techniques, page 158).

Simplicity

In bygone days, a woman's wedding trousseau was filled with linen kerchiefs, petticoats, and underskirts in natural shades of cream and off white; later, baby clothes were made from these used textiles. This afghan pays homage to that tradition. Solid squares of double crochet are framed with an openwork mesh of filet crochet, mimicking the effect of drawn-work embroidery on white linen handkerchiefs.

Finished Measurements

30" wide x 36" long

Yarn

Berroco Comfort DK (50% super fine nylon / 50% super fine acrylic; 50 grams / 178 yards): 15 skeins #2702 Pearl

Crochet Hook

Crochet hook size US F/5 (3.75 mm)
Change hook size if necessary to obtain correct gauge.

Gauge

21 sts and 10 rows = 4" (10 cm) in pattern stitch

Blanket

Ch 154.

Row 1: Sc in 2nd ch from hook and in each ch across–153 sts, turn.

Row 2: Ch 1, sc in each sc to end, turn.

Row 3: Ch 4 (counts as 1 dc and ch 1), dc in 3rd sc, *ch 1, sk 1 sc, dc in next sc, repeat from * to end, turn.

Row 4: Ch 3 (counts as dc), dc in ch-1 sp, [dc in next dc, dc in ch-1 sp] 10 times, *[dc in next dc, sk 1 ch, ch 1] twice, [dc in next dc, dc in next ch-1 sp] 11 times; repeat from * 5 times, dc in 3rd ch, turn.

Rows 5-17: Ch 3 (counts as dc), sk first dc, dc in next 22 dc, *ch 1, dc in dc, ch 1, dc in next 23 dc; repeat from * 5 times.

Row 18: Ch 4 (counts as 1 dc and ch 1), dc in 3rd dc, *ch 1, sk 1 dc, dc in next dc; repeat from * to end.

Rows 19-108: Repeat Rows 4-18 six times.

Row 109: Ch 1, sc in each dc and ch-1 sp to end, turn.

Row 110: Ch 1, sc in each sc to end. Fasten off.

Finishing

SIDE EDGING

With RS facing and beginning at corner, join yarn with a dc.

Row 1: *Ch 1, sk 1 st, dc in next st; repeat from * to end, turn.

Row 2: Ch 1, sc in each dc and ch-1 sp to end, turn.

Row 3: Ch 1, sc in each sc to end, turn. Fasten off.

Repeat for second side edge.

Block lightly (see Special Techniques, page 158).

Square Off

Though this afghan is composed of squares within squares, each motif is slightly different, with five unique combinations repeated using different color combinations. The varied sizes of the internal squares play with proportion, adding a wealth of visual interest. The neutral colors create a soothing palette, while textural crochet stitches make the squares stand out from one another.

Finished Measurements

60" wide x 72" long

Yarn

Berroco Comfort (50% super fine nylon / 50% super fine acrylic; 100 grams / 210 yards): 6 skeins #9720 Hummus (A); 5 skeins #9701 Ivory (B); 4 skeins each #9716 Chambray (C) and #9727 Spanish Brown (D); 3 skeins #9741 Bitter Sweet (E)

Crochet Hook

Crochet hook size US H/8 (5 mm)
Change hook size if necessary to obtain correct gauge.

Gauge

14 sts and 8 rows = 4" (10 cm) in Double Crochet (dc)

Abbreviations

MB (Make Bobble): Yo and pull up a loop in next st, yo and draw through 2 loops on hook, *yo and pull up a loop in same st, yo and draw through 2 loops on hook; repeat from * 4 times, yo and draw through all loops on hook.

Stitch Pattern

BOBBLE STITCH (multiple of 4 sts + 3 + 1 ch; 2-row repeat)
Set-Up Row: Dc in 3rd ch from hook, and in each ch across, turn.
Row 1: Ch 3 (counts as dc), skip first dc, MB in next dc, *dc in next 3 dc, MB in next dc; repeat from * to last dc, dc in last dc, turn.
Row 2: Ch 3 (counts as dc), skip first dc, dc in Bobble, 1 dc, *MB in next dc, 3 dc; repeat from *, ending last dc in top of ch, turn.
Repeat Rows 1 and 2 for Bobble Stitch.

Afghan

SQUARE A (make 6)
Using C, ch 5, join with a sl st to form ring.
Rnd 1: Ch 3 (counts as dc), work 11 dc into ring, join with a sl st in top of ch-3–12 sts.
Rnd 2: Ch 3 (always counts as dc), dc in next dc, *3 dc in next dc (corner), dc in next 2 dc; repeat from * twice, 3 dc in next dc (corner), sl st in top of ch-3–20 sts.
Rnd 3: Ch 3, 2 dc, *3 dc in center dc of corner, 4 dc; repeat from * twice, 3 dc in center dc of corner, 1 dc, sl st in top of ch-3–28 sts.
Rnd 4: Change to A, ch 3, 3 dc, *3 dc in center dc of corner, 6 dc; repeat from * twice, 3 dc in center dc of corner, 2 dc, sl st in top of ch-3–36 sts.

Rnd 5: Ch 3, 4 dc, *3 dc in center dc of corner, 8 dc; repeat from * twice, 3 dc in center dc of corner, 3 dc, sl st in top of ch-3–44 sts.

Rnd 6: Change to E, ch 3, 5 dc, *3 dc in center dc of corner, 10 dc; repeat from * twice, 3 dc in center dc of corner, 4 dc, sl st in top of ch-3–52 sts.

Rnd 7: Ch 3, 6 dc, *3 dc in center dc of corner, 12 dc; repeat from * twice, 3 dc in center dc of corner, 5 dc, sl st in top of ch-3–60 sts.

Rnd 8: Ch 3, 7 dc, *3 dc in center dc of corner, 14 dc; repeat from * twice, 3 dc in center dc of corner, 6 dc, sl st in top of ch-3–68 sts.

Rnd 9: Ch 3, 8 dc, *3 dc in center dc of corner, 16 dc; repeat from * twice, 3 dc in center dc of corner, 7 dc, sl st in top of ch-3–76 sts.

Rnd 10: Change to A, ch 3, 9 dc, *3 dc in corner, 18 dc; repeat from * twice, end 3 sc in corner, 8 dc, sl st on top of ch-3–84 sts.

Rnd 11: Ch 3, 2 dc, [MB, 3 dc] twice, *3 dc in corner, [3 dc, MB] 5 times; repeat from * twice, end 3 dc in corner, 2 dc, MB, 3 dc, MB, 2 dc, sl st in top of ch-3–92 sts.

Rnd 12: Ch 3, [MB, 3 dc] twice, MB, 2 dc, *3 dc in corner, 2 dc, [MB, 3 dc] 5 times; repeat from * twice, end 3 dc in corner, 1 dc, [MB, 3 dc] twice, 1dc, sl st in top of ch-3–100 sts.

Rnd 13: Ch 3, 2 dc, [MB, 3 dc] twice, MB, 1 dc, *3 dc in corner, 1 dc, [MB, 3 dc] 5 times, MB, 2 dc; repeat from * twice, end 3 dc in corner, [MB, 3 dc] twice, MB, 2 dc, sl st in top of ch-3–108 sts.

Rnd 14: Ch 3, 13 dc, *3 dc in corner, 26 dc; repeat from * twice, end 3 dc in corner, 12 dc, sl st in top of ch-3–116 sts.

Rnd 15: Ch 3, 14 dc, *3 dc in corner, 28 dc; repeat from * twice, end 3 dc in corner, 13 dc, sl st in top of ch-3–124 sts. Fasten off.

SQUARE B (make 6)
Using B, ch 16. Begin Bobble st; work even for 8 rows. Fasten off.

Rnd 1: Change to D. *Work 12 dc across one side of Square, work 3 dc in corner; repeat from * around Square, sl st in first dc–60 sts.

Rnds 2-9: Ch 3 (counts as dc), dc in each dc around, working 3 dc in each corner–124 sts. Fasten off.

ASSEMBLY DIAGRAM

A	B	C	D	E
D	E	A	B	C
B	C	D	E	A
E	A	B	C	D
C	D	E	A	B
A	B	C	D	E

SQUARE C (make 6)

Using C, ch 5, join with a sl st to form ring.

Rnd 1: Ch 3 (counts as dc), work 11 dc into ring, join with a sl st in top of ch-3–12 sts.

Rnd 2: Ch 3 (always counts as dc), dc in next dc, *3 dc in next dc (corner made), dc in next 2 dc; repeat from * twice, 3 dc in next dc (corner made), sl st in top of ch-3–20 sts.

Rnd 3: Ch 3, 2 dc, *3 dc in center dc of corner, 4 dc; repeat from * twice, 3 dc in center dc of corner, 1 dc, sl st in top of ch-3–28 sts.

Rnd 4: Ch 3, 3 dc, *3 dc in center dc of corner, 6 dc; repeat from * twice, 3 dc in center dc of corner, 2 dc, sl st in top of ch-3–36 sts.

Rnd 5: Ch 3, 4 dc, *3 dc in center dc of corner, 8 dc; repeat from * twice, 3 dc in center dc of corner, 3 dc, sl st in top of ch-3–44 sts.

Rnd 6: Ch 3, 5 dc, *3 dc in center dc of corner, 10 dc; repeat from * twice, 3 dc in center dc of corner, 4 dc, sl st in top of ch-3–52 sts.

Rnd 7: Ch 3, 6 dc, *3 dc in center dc of corner, 12 dc; repeat from * twice, 3 dc in center dc of corner, 5 dc, sl st in top of ch-3–60 sts.

Rnd 8: Ch 3, 7 dc, *3 dc in center dc of corner, 14 dc; repeat from * twice, 3 dc in center dc of corner, 6 dc, sl st in top of ch-3–68 sts.

Rnd 9: Ch 3, 8 dc, *3 dc in center dc of corner, 16 dc; repeat from * twice, 3 dc in center dc of corner, 7 dc, sl st in top of ch-3–76 sts.

Rnd 10: Change to A. Ch 3, 9 dc, *3 dc in center dc of corner, 18 dc; repeat from * twice, 3 dc in center dc of corner, 8 dc, sl st in top of ch-3–84 sts.

Rnd 11: Ch 3, 2 dc, MB, 3 dc, MB, 3 dc, *3 dc in corner, [3 dc, MB] 5 times; repeat from * twice, end 3 dc in corner, 2 dc, MB, 3 dc, MB, 2 dc, sl st in top of ch-3–92 sts.

Rnd 12: Ch 3, [MB, 3 dc] twice, MB, 2 dc, *3 dc in corner, 2 dc [MB, 3 dc] 5 times; repeat from * twice, end 3 dc in corner, 1 dc, [MB, 3 dc] twice, 1dc, sl st in top of ch-3–100 sts.

Rnd 13: Change to E. Ch 3, 12 dc, *3 dc in corner, 24 dc; repeat from * twice, end 3 dc in corner, 11 dc, sl st in top of ch-3–108 sts.

Rnd 14: Ch 3, 13 dc, *3 dc in corner, 26 dc; repeat from * twice, end 3 dc in corner, 12 dc, sl st in top of ch-3–116 sts.

Rnd 15: Ch 3, 14 dc, *3 dc in corner, 28 dc; repeat from * twice, end 3 dc in corner, 13 dc, sl st in top of ch-3–124 sts. Fasten off.

SQUARE D (make 6)

Using E, ch 28. Begin Bobble st; work even for 17 rows. Fasten off.

Rnd 1: Change to B. *Work 18 dc across one side of square, work 3 dc in corner; repeat from * around Square, sl st in first dc–84 sts.

Rnds 2-6: Ch 3 (counts as dc), dc in each dc around, working 3 dc in each corner–124 sts. Fasten off.

SQUARE E (make 6)

Using C, ch 5, join with a sl st to form ring.

Rnd 1: Ch 3 (counts as dc), work 11 dc into ring, join with a sl st in top of ch-3–12 sts.

Rnd 2: Ch 3 (always counts as dc), dc in next dc, *3 dc in next dc (corner made), dc in next 2 dc; repeat from * twice, 3 dc in next dc (corner made), sl st in top of ch-3–20 sts.

Rnd 3: Ch 3, 2 dc, *3 dc in center dc of corner, 4 dc; repeat from * twice, 3 dc in center dc of corner, 1 dc, sl st in top of ch-3–28 sts.

Rnd 4: Change to A. Ch 3, 3 dc, *3 dc in corner, 6 dc; repeat from * twice, end 3 dc in corner, 2 dc, sl st in top of ch-3–36 sts.

Rnd 5: Ch 3, 4 dc, *3 dc in corner, 3 dc, MB, 4 dc; repeat from * twice, end 3 dc in corner, 2 dc, MB, sl st in top of ch-3–44 sts.

Rnd 6: Ch 3, 1 dc, MB, 3 dc, *3 dc in corner, 2 dc, [MB, 3 dc] twice; repeat from * twice, end 3 dc in corner, 1 dc, MB, 2 dc, sl st in top of ch-3–52 sts.

Rnd 7: Ch 3, 3 dc, MB, 2 dc, *3 dc in corner, 1 dc, [MB, 3 dc] twice, MB, 2 dc: repeat from *, end 3 dc in corner, MB, 3 dc, MB, sl st in top of ch-3–60 sts.

Rnd 8: Ch 3, 1 dc, MB, 3 dc, MB, 1 dc, *3 dc in corner, [MB, 3 dc] 3 times, MB, 1 dc; repeat from * twice, end 3 dc in corner, 3 dc, MB, 2 dc, sl st to top of ch-3–68 sts.

Rnd 9: Ch 3, 3 dc, MB, 3 dc, MB, *3 dc in corner, [3 dc, MB] 4 times; repeat from * twice, end 3 dc in corner, 2 dc, MB, 3 dc, MB, sl st in top of ch-3–76 sts.

Rnd 10: Change to D. Ch 3, 9 dc, *3 dc in corner, 18 dc; repeat from * twice, end 3 dc in corner, 8 dc, sl st in top of ch-3–84 sts.

Rnd 11: Ch 3, 10 dc, *3 dc in corner, 20 dc; repeat from * twice, end 3 dc in corner, 9 dc, sl st in top of ch-3–92 sts.

Rnd 12: Ch 3, 11 dc, *3 dc in corner, 22 dc; repeat from * twice, end 3 dc in corner, 10 dc, sl st in top of ch-3–100 sts.

Rnd 13: Change to C. Ch 3, 12 dc, *3 dc in corner, 24 dc; repeat from * twice, end 3 dc in corner, 11 dc, sl st in top of ch-3–108 sts.

Rnd 14: Ch 3, 13 dc, *3 dc in corner, 26 dc; repeat from * twice, end 3 dc in corner, 12 dc, sl st in top of ch-3–116 sts.

Rnd 15: Ch 3, 14 dc, *3 dc in corner, 28 dc; repeat from * twice, end 3 dc in corner, 13 dc, sl st in top of ch-3–124 sts.

Finishing

Sew Squares together following Assembly Diagram.
Block lightly (see Special Techniques, page 158).

Still Life

Abstract blossoms abound in this knitted equivalent of a still-life painting, complete with a mitered frame of creamy white garter stitch. The intarsia is worked with separate bobbins for each color. The experience is much like painting by numbers, but with yarn.

Finished Measurements
42" wide x 45" long

Yarn
Berroco Comfort (50% super fine nylon / 50% super fine acrylic; 100 grams / 210 yards): 5 skeins #9701 Ivory (A); 1 skein each #9758 Crypto Crystalline (B), #9716 Chambray (C), #9723 Rosebud (D), #9730 Teaberry (E), #9728 Raspberry Sorbet (F), #9739 Grape Jelly (G), #9726 Cornflower (H), #9722 Purple (I), #9754 Rabe (J), #9721 Sprig (K), #9742 Pimpernel (L), #9780 Dried Plum (M), #9745 Filbert (N), #9760 Beet Root (O), #9729 Smokestack (P), #9713 Dusk (Q), #9748 Aunt Martha Green (R), #9720 Hummus (S), #9703 Barley (T), and #9762 Spruce (U)

Needles
One 36" (90 cm) long or longer circular (circ) needle size US 8 (5 mm)
One 36" (90 cm) long or longer circular needle size US 7 (4.5 mm)
Change needle size if necessary to obtain correct gauge.

Gauge
20 sts and 28 rows = 4" (10 cm) over Still Life Chart

Throw
Using larger needle, CO 160 sts. Begin Still Life Chart; work until entire Chart is complete. BO all sts.

Finishing
Side Edging: With RS facing, using circ needle and A, pick up and knit 180 sts evenly spaced along side edge.
Rows 1-3: Knit.
Row 4: K1, M1, knit to last st, M1, k1–182 sts.
Repeat Rows 1-4 nine times–200 sts. BO all sts.
Repeat for opposite side.
Bottom Edging: With RS facing, using smaller needle and A, pick up and knit 164 sts evenly spaced along bottom edge. Work Rows 1-4 of Side Edging 10 times–184 sts. BO all sts.
Repeat for top edge. Sew corner seams.
Block lightly (see Special Techniques, page 158).

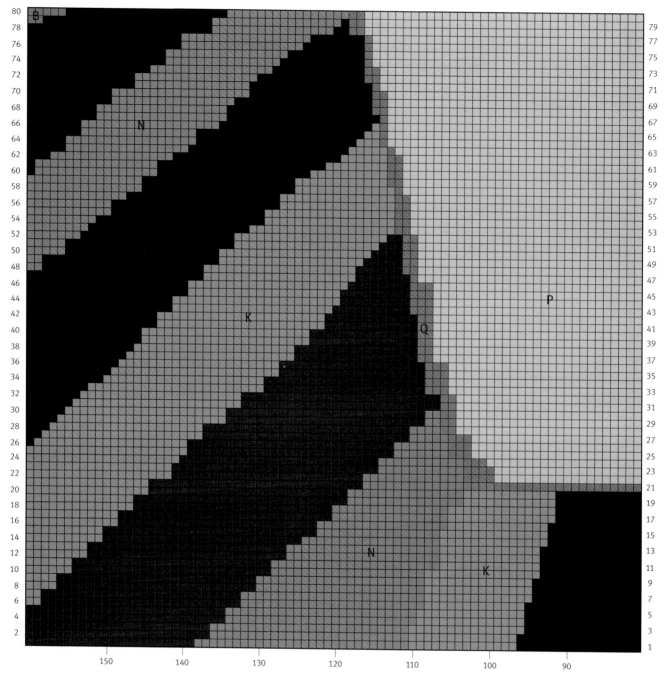

KEY

Knit on RS, purl on WS.

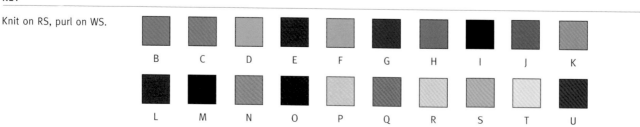

B C D E F G H I J K

L M N O P Q R S T U

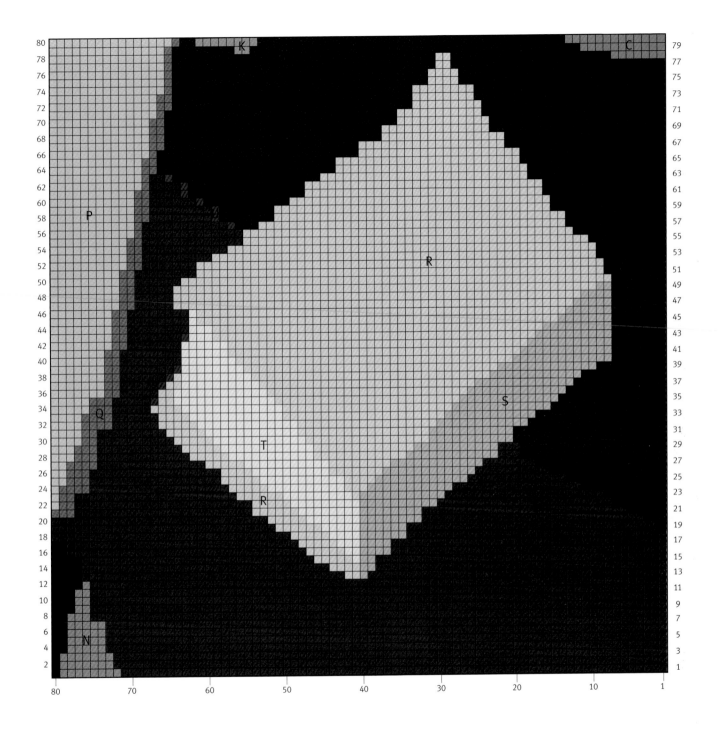

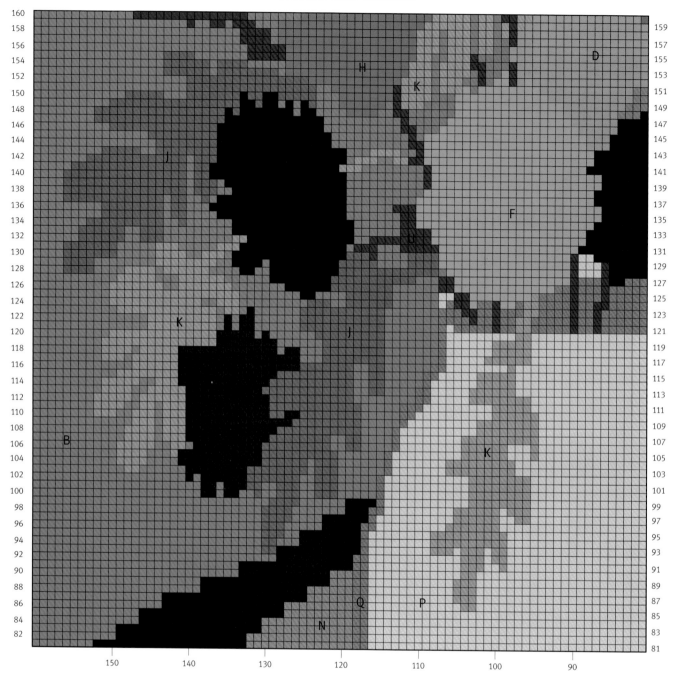

KEY

Knit on RS, purl on WS.

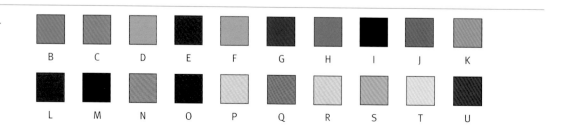

B   C   D   E   F   G   H   I   J   K

L   M   N   O   P   Q   R   S   T   U

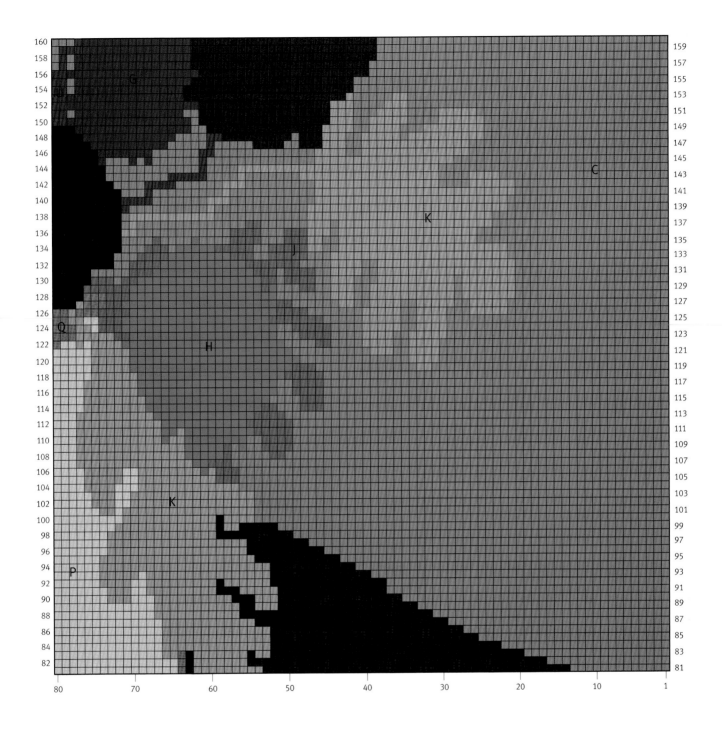

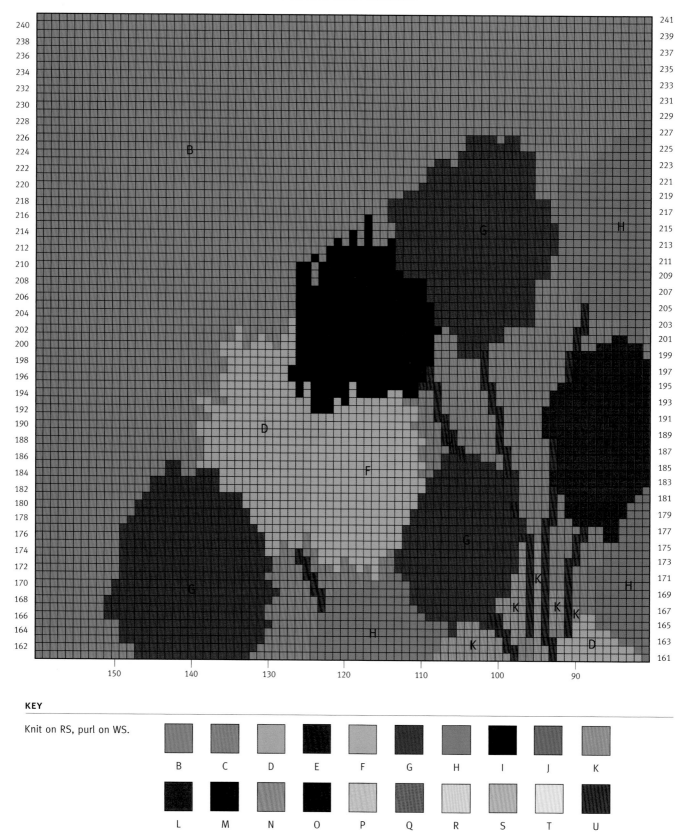

KEY

Knit on RS, purl on WS.

B C D E F G H I J K

L M N O P Q R S T U

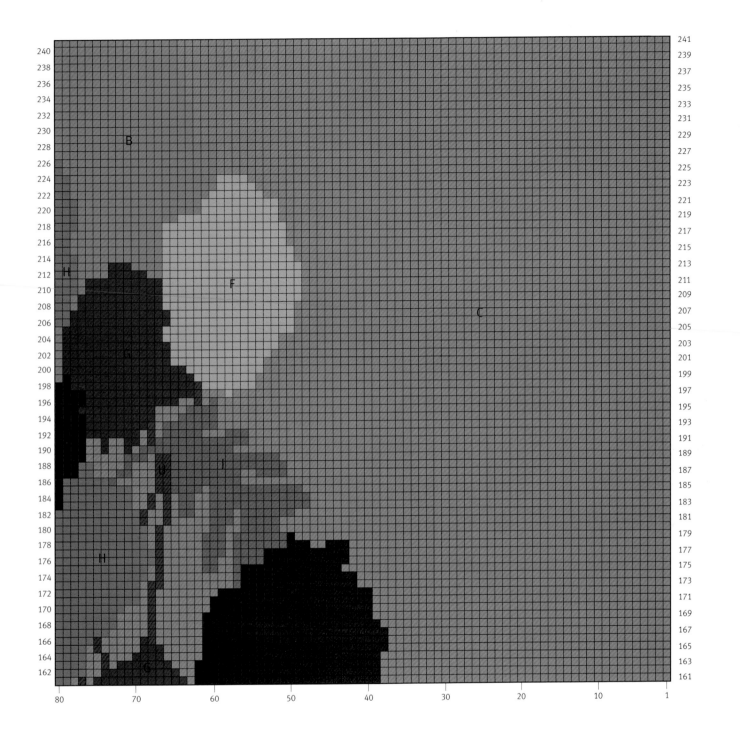

Swirl

Hexagons fit together like the cells of a honeycomb in this brightly colored baby blanket. The spirals are created by decreasing at the same spot on every round, and are further accented by eyelets, giving the whole afghan a sense of movement. For a more traditional baby gift, change the colors to all white, or try a variety of softer shades.

Finished Measurements
42" wide x 44" long

Yarn
Berroco Comfort (50% super fine nylon / 50% super fine acrylic; 100 grams / 210 yards): 2 skeins each #9735 Delft Blue (A), #9726 Cornflower (B), and #9740 Seedling (C); 1 skein each #9743 Goldenrod (D) and #9732 Primary Yellow (E)

Needles
One 16" (40 cm) long circular (circ) needle size US 8 (5 mm)
One set of five double-pointed needles (dpn) size US 8 (5 mm)
Change needle size if necessary to obtain correct gauge.

Notions
Stitch markers

Gauge
20 sts and 24 rows = 4" (10 cm) in Seed stitch

Stitch Pattern
SEED STITCH (odd number of sts; 1-row repeat)
All Rows: K1, *p1, k1; repeat from * to end.

Afghan
Note: You may begin at any point in the Assembly Diagram for the First Hexagon. Pick the center Hexagon to start with and work out in concentric rings from there, or pick a Hexagon on the outside edge and work in toward the center. Once you've worked the First Hexagon, you will pick up sts along one edge of it for the first edge of the next Hexagon, then cast on sts for the remaining edges. All of the following Hexagons will be worked off of the preceding Hexagons. Each Hexagon has 120 sts, 20 sts per side. You will always pick up 20 sts per side for each side of adjacent Hexagons, then cast on enough additional sts to get to 120 sts.

FIRST HEXAGON
Using circ needle and color of your choice, CO 120 sts, placing markers every 20 sts. Join and place a distinctive marker at beginning of rnd.
Note: Change to dpns when necessary for number of sts on needle.
Rnd 1 (RS): *P2, [k1, p1] 7 times, ssk, yo, ssk; repeat from * to end–114 sts remain.
Rnd 2: *P1, [k1, p1] 7 times, ssk, yo, ssk; repeat from * to end–108 sts remain.
Rnd 3: *P2, [k1, p1] 6 times, ssk, yo, ssk; repeat from * to end–102 sts remain.
Rnd 4: *P1, [k1, p1] 6 times, ssk, yo, ssk; repeat from * to end–96 sts remain.
Rnd 5: *P2, [k1, p1] 5 times, ssk, yo, ssk; repeat from * to end–90 sts remain.
Rnd 6: *P1, [k1, p1] 5 times, ssk, yo, ssk; repeat from * to end–84 sts remain.

ASSEMBLY DIAGRAM

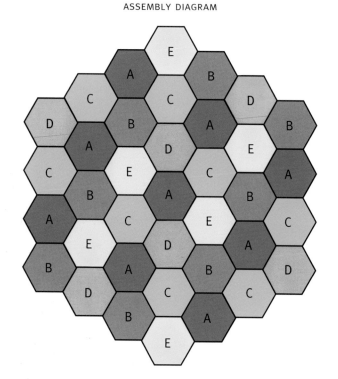

Rnd 7: *P2, [k1, p1] 4 times, ssk, yo, ssk; repeat from * to end–78 sts remain.

Rnd 8: *P1, [k1, p1] 4 times, ssk, yo, ssk; repeat from * to end–72 sts remain.

Rnd 9: *P2, [k1, p1] 3 times, ssk, yo, ssk; repeat from * to end–66 sts remain.

Rnd 10: *P1, [k1, p1] 3 times, ssk, yo, ssk; repeat from * to end–60 sts remain.

Rnd 11: *P2, [k1, p1] 2 times, ssk, yo, ssk; repeat from * to end–54 sts remain.

Rnd 12: *P1, [k1, p1] 2 times, ssk, yo, ssk; repeat from * to end–48 sts remain.

Rnd 13: *P2, k1, p1, ssk, yo, ssk; repeat from * to end–42 sts remain.

Rnd 14: *P1, k1, p1, ssk, yo, ssk; repeat from * to end–36 sts remain.

Rnd 15: *P2, ssk, yo, ssk; repeat from * to end–30 sts remain.

Rnd 16: *P1, ssk, yo, ssk; repeat from * to end–24 sts remain.

Rnd 17: *Ssk, yo, ssk; repeat from * to end–18 sts remain.

Rnd 18: *K1, ssk; repeat from * to end–12 sts remain.

Rnd 19: [Ssk] 6 times–6 sts remain. BO.

NEXT HEXAGON

Using color for next Hexagon in Assembly Diagram, pick up and knit 20 sts from First Hexagon. CO 100 sts for remaining sides, placing markers every 20 sts–120 sts. Complete as for First Hexagon.

REMAINING HEXAGONS

Using color for next Hexagon in Assembly Diagram, pick up and knit 20 sts per side for each adjacent 1 or more previous Hexagons, cast on additional sts for remaining sides to get to 120 sts, placing markers every 20 sts. Complete as for First Hexagon.

Finishing

Block lightly (see Special Techniques, page 158).

Trapper

Influenced by the Indian horse blankets that were popular in the late 1960s, this hippie-chic afghan is worked in easy double crochet stripes; the distance between stripes is varied at one end for visual interest. The result is a good match for all sorts of environments—from a teenager's room to a log cabin to a modern loft.

Finished Measurements
50" wide x 60" long

Yarn
Berroco Comfort DK (50% super fine nylon / 50% super fine acrylic; 50 grams / 178 yards): 11 skeins #2703 Barley (A); 10 skeins #2741 Bitter Sweet (B)

Crochet Hook
Crochet hook size US F/5 (3.75 mm)
Change hook size if necessary to obtain correct gauge.

Gauge
16 sts and 10 rows = 4" (10 cm) in Double Crochet (dc)

Stitch Patterns
DOUBLE CROCHET (dc) (any number of sts + 1 ch; 1 row repeat)
Set-Up Row: Dc in 4th ch from hook, dc in each ch across, turn.
All Rows: Ch 3 (counts as dc), skip first dc, dc in each dc across, turn.

STRIPE SEQUENCE
Work 2 rows B, 10 rows A, 4 rows B, 10 rows A, *2 rows B, then 4 rows A; repeat from * for Stripe Sequence.

Throw
Using A, ch 203. Begin Double Crochet (dc); work even for 2 rows. Continuing in dc, begin Stripe Sequence; work even until piece measures 60" from the beginning, ending with 2 rows B.

Finishing
Block lightly (see Special Techniques, page 158).

Ukrainian Tiles

Complex geometric patterns have been common in textiles and traditional home crafts throughout the world for centuries. The two-tone geometric patterns used here were inspired by classic Eastern European textiles as well as the elaborate patterns used to decorate Ukrainian Easter eggs. The snowflakes around the afghan's seed-stitch border are created with a clever and easy embroidery technique that calls for sewing X's in the contrasting color atop the seed-stitch bumps.

Finished Measurements
40" wide x 53" long

Yarn
Berroco Comfort (50% super fine nylon / 50% super fine acrylic; 100 grams / 210 yards): 10 skeins each #9755 Wild Cherry (A) and #9703 Barley (B)

Needles
One 36" (90 cm) long or longer circular (circ) needle size US 8 (5 mm)
Change needle size if necessary to obtain correct gauge.

Notions
Stitch markers

Gauge
21 sts and 22 rows = 4" (10 cm) in Ukrainian Tiles Pattern from Chart

Afghan
CENTER PANEL
Using A, CO 170 sts. Purl 1 row.

Sequence 1 (RS): *Work 34 sts from Ukrainian Tiles Pattern Chart in Colorway 1, place marker (pm), work 34 sts from Chart in Colorway 2, pm; repeat from * once, work last 34 sts from Chart in Colorway 1. Work even until Row 28 is complete.

Sequence 2 (RS): *Work Chart in Colorway 2 to next marker, work Chart in Colorway 1 to next marker; repeat from * once, work Chart to end in Colorway 2. Work even until Row 28 is complete.

Repeat Sequences 1 and 2 twice, then repeat Sequence 1 once. BO all sts.

Finishing
SIDE EDGING
With RS facing, using circ needle and B, pick up and knit 161 sts evenly spaced along side edge of afghan.

Rows 1 (WS)-7: Using B, k1, *p1, k1; repeat from * to end.

Row 8: K1 A, *p1 B [carrying nonworking yarn (A) across front of this st to create float on RS], k1 A; repeat from * to end.

Row 9: P1 B, *k1 B [carrying nonworking yarn (A) across back of this st to create float on RS, then place A to front], p1 B; repeat from * to end.

Rows 10-26: Using B, p1, *k1, p1; repeat from * to end.

Rows 27 and 28: Change to A. Knit.

Row 29: Change to B. Knit.

Rows 30 and 32: K1 A, *p1 B, k1 A; repeat from * to end.

Row 31: K1 B, *p1 A, k1 B; repeat from * to end.

UKRAINIAN TILES PATTERN CHART

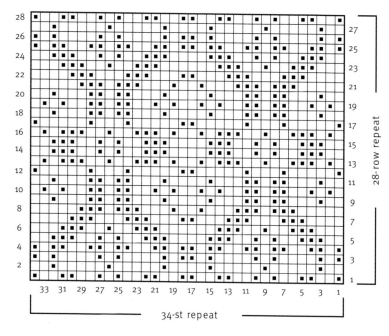

28-row repeat

34-st repeat

KEY

Knit on RS, purl on WS.

Colorway 1

☐ A

⊡ B

Colorway 2

☐ B

⊡ A

✖ Cross st (p. 157)

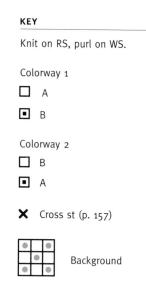

Background

EMBROIDERY CHART

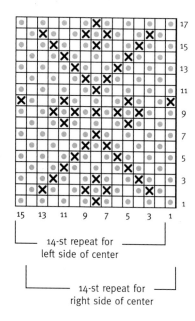

14-st repeat for
left side of center

14-st repeat for
right side of center

Row 33: Change to B. Purl.

Rows 34 and 35: Change to A. Knit.

BO all sts.

Repeat for opposite edge.

BOTTOM EDGING

With RS facing, using circ needle and A, pick up and knit 199 sts evenly spaced along bottom edge of afghan.

Row 1 (WS): Purl.

Rows 2 and 4: K1 A, *p1 B, k1 A; repeat from * to end.

Rows 3 and 5: K1 B, *p1 A, k1 B; repeat from * to end.

Row 6: Change to A. Knit.

Row 7: Purl.

Row 8: Change to B. Knit.

Row 9: P1 B, *k1 A, p1 B; repeat from * to end.

Row 10: P1 A, *k1 B, p1 A; repeat from * to end.

Row 11: Change to A. Purl.

Row 12: Knit.

Rows 13 and 14: K1 A, *p1 B, k1 A; repeat from * to end.

Row 15: P1 B, k1 A, *p1 B [carrying nonworking yarn (A) across back of this st to create float on RS], k1 A; repeat from * to last st, p1 B.

Row 16: P1 A, *k1 B, p1 A; repeat from * to end.

Rows 17 and 18: Repeat Rows 11 and 12.

Rows 19-53: Work Rows 1-35 of Side Edging.

BO all sts.

Repeat for top edge.

Embroidery: On all sides of afghan, find center knit st of Row 18 of Side Edging. Follow Embroidery Chart for placement of cross sts, repeating out from center, working partial motifs at ends if desired.

Final Edging: With RS facing, using circ needle and A, pick up and knit approximately 880 sts evenly spaced around entire edge of afghan. Join for working in the rnd; pm for beginning of rnd. Knit 1 rnd. Using 1 strand each of A and B held together, BO all sts.

Block lightly (see Special Techniques, page 158).

Danish Modern

This afghan is inspired by the rectilinear lines of Danish modern furniture. The logical alternation of color makes the stranded colorwork easy to memorize, and the chunky gauge makes it quick to knit. Worked in blocks, this is the kind of project that can travel with you; a week of commuting on the train and you could have a new afghan ready for your sofa.

Finished Measurements
42" wide x 60" long

Yarn
Berroco Comfort Chunky (50% super fine nylon / 50% super fine acrylic; 100 grams / 150 yards): 7 skeins #5734 Liquorice (A); 4 skeins #5747 Cadet (B); 3 skeins #5703 Barley (C)

Needles
One pair straight needles size US 10½ (6.5 mm)
Change needle size if necessary to obtain correct gauge.

Gauge
16 sts and 18 rows = 4" (10 cm) in Stockinette stitch (St st)

Throw

MOTIF 1 (make 15)
Using A, CO 24 sts. Purl 2 rows. Change to Chart 1, Colorway 1. Work Rows 1-22 once. Change to A; knit 2 rows. Change to C; knit 1 row, purl 1 row. Change to Chart 1, Colorway 2. Work Rows 1-22 once. Change to C; knit 2 rows. BO all sts.

MOTIF 2 (make 10)
Using B, CO 24 sts. Purl 2 rows. Change to Chart 2, Colorway 3. Work Rows 1-22 once. Change to B; knit 2 rows. Change to A; knit 1 row, purl 1 row. Change to Chart 2, Colorway 4. Work Rows 1-22 once. Change to A; knit 2 rows. BO all sts.

MOTIF 3 (make 5)
Using B, CO 27 sts.
Row 1 (RS): Work 3 sts in Garter st (knit every row), work to end as for Motif 2.
Row 2: Work to last 3 sts, work in Garter st to end.
Work even until instructions for Motif 2 have been completed.

MOTIF 4 (make 5)
Using B, CO 27 sts.
Row 1 (RS): Work as for Motif 2 to last 3 sts, work in Garter st to end.
Row 2: Work 3 sts in Garter st, work to end.
Work even until instructions for Motif 2 have been completed.

Finishing
Sew Motifs together following Assembly Diagram.
Block lightly (see Special Techniques, page 158).

CHART 1

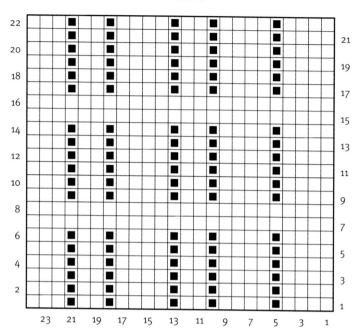

Knit on RS, purl on WS.

Colorway 1	Colorway 2	Colorway 3	Colorway 4
☐ A	☐ C	☐ B	☐ A
■ C	■ A	■ A	■ B

CHART 2

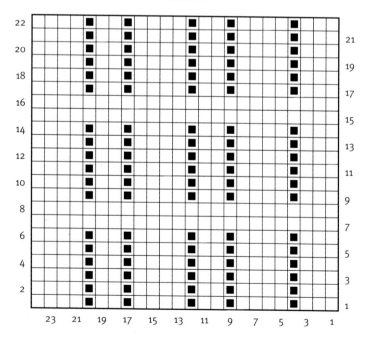

ASSEMBLY DIAGRAM

4	1	2	1	2	1	3
4	1	2	1	2	1	3
4	1	2	1	2	1	3
4	1	2	1	2	1	3
4	1	2	1	2	1	3

Nordic Holiday

The strong palette of black, white, and red is traditional in northern European dress and household textiles, but looks modern in this bold, graphic design. Each square is made with an easy, textured stripe pattern, which is then crowned with a blaze of red. When assembled, the squares form red stair steps. Instructions are given for a large afghan (as shown on page 126) and a smaller throw-sized version.

Finished Measurements
Large Afghan: 62" wide x 74" long
Small Afghan: 50" wide x 62" long
Note: Numbers for Large Afghan are given first, and numbers for Small Afghan are given in parentheses. Where only one number is given, it applies to both sizes.

Yarn
Berroco Comfort (50% super fine nylon / 50% super fine acrylic; 100 grams / 210 yards): 5 (3) skeins #9755 Wild Cherry (A); 10 (7) skeins #9734 Liquorice (B); 11 (8) skeins #9701 Ivory (C)

Needles
One pair straight needles size US 8 (5 mm)
One 36" (90 cm) long or longer circular (circ) needle size US 8 (5 mm)
Change needle size if necessary to obtain correct gauge.

Gauge
20 sts and 27 rows = 4" (10 cm) in Stockinette stitch (St st)

Afghan

SQUARES [make 99 (63)]

Using A, CO 30 sts.

Rows 1 (RS)-6: Knit.

Rows 7 and 8: Change to B. Knit.

Note: Do not cut yarn; carry colors not in use up side edge of work.

Rows 9 and 10: *K1, p1; repeat from * to end.

Rows 11 and 12: *P1, k1; repeat from * to end.

Row 13: Change to C. *K1, p1; repeat from * to end.

Row 14: Purl.

Rows 15 and 16: Change to B. *P1, k1; repeat from * to end.

Rows 17 and 18: Change to C. Purl.

Rows 19 and 20: Change to B. *K1, p1; repeat from * to end.

Row 21: Change to C. *P1, k1; repeat from * to end.

Rows 22, 24, and 26: Purl.

Rows 23 and 25: Knit.

Rows 27 and 28: Change to B. *K1, p1; repeat from * to end.

Rows 29 and 30: *P1, k1; repeat from * to end.

Rows 31 and 32: *K1, p1; repeat from * to end.

Rows 33 and 34: Change to A. *P1, k1; repeat from * to end.

Rows 35 and 36: Change to B. *K1, p1; repeat from * to end.

Rows 37 and 38: Change to C. Purl.

Rows 39 and 40: Change to B, *P1, k1; repeat from * to end.

Row 41: Change to C. *K1, p1; repeat from * to end.

Row 42: Purl.

Row 43: Knit.

Row 44: Purl.

BO all sts.

Finishing

With RS facing, sew Squares together following Assembly Diagram, with all seams to WS.

Side Edging: With RS facing, using circ needle and B, pick up and knit 299 (245) sts evenly spaced along side edge. Begin Garter St (knit every row); work even for 1". Change to C; work even for 3". BO all sts. Repeat for second side.

Bottom Edging: With RS facing, using circ needle and B, pick up and knit 281 (227) sts evenly spaced along bottom edge. Begin Garter st; work even for 1". Change to C and work even for 3". BO all sts. Repeat for top edge.

Block lightly (see Special Techniques, page 158).

ASSEMBLY DIAGRAM

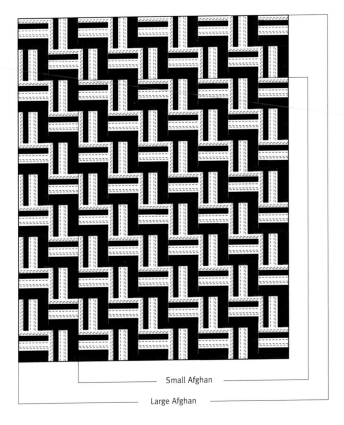

Small Afghan

Large Afghan

ZigZag

The simple geometric design of this two-color afghan is a nice fit for all kinds of rooms. It can work as a foil against brightly colored upholstery or blend in beautifully with masculine or modern furniture. If you work the two-stranded colorwork with one color of yarn in each hand, your work will progress very quickly.

Finished Measurements

44" wide x 60" long, not including Fringe

Yarn

Berroco Comfort Chunky (50% super fine nylon / 50% super fine acrylic; 100 grams / 150 yards): 8 skeins each #5734 Liquorice (A) and #5713 Dusk (B)

Needles

One 36" (90 cm) long or longer circular (circ) needle size US 10½ (6.5 mm)
Change needle size if necessary to obtain correct gauge.

Notions

Crochet hook size US J/10 (6 mm)

Gauge

16 sts and 18 rows = 4" in ZigZag Pattern from Chart

Throw

Using A, CO 174 sts. Begin ZigZag Pattern from Chart. Work even until throw measures 60" from the beginning. BO all sts.

Finishing

LOOPED FRINGE

Using crochet hook and A, join with sl st in corner and work 1 rnd of sc evenly around entire throw, working 3 sc in each corner. Do not turn. Ch 1, sc in first sc, *yo, pull loop through and up to measure 2", take hook out of st and sc in next sc, being careful to keep Fringe even; repeat from * around entire throw. Sl st to first ch. Fasten off.
Block lightly (see Special Techniques, page 158).

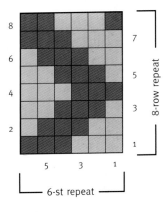

ZIGZAG PATTERN

8-row repeat

6-st repeat

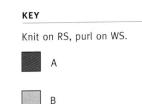

KEY

Knit on RS, purl on WS.

A

B

Malian Lattice

From a distance, this striking black-and-white lattice design looks like gingham. But when you examine it more closely, you see that the diamonds are composed of labyrinthine colorwork and solid black diamonds. The overall pattern is loosely based on the design of mud cloth weavings from Mali and other regions in Africa.

Finished Measurements

44" wide x 65" long

Yarn

Berroco Comfort Chunky (50% super fine nylon / 50% super fine acrylic; 100 grams / 150 yards): 8 skeins each #5734 Liquorice (A) and #5703 Barley (B)

Needles

One 36" (90 cm) long or longer circular (circ) needle size US 10½ (6.5 mm)
Change needle size if necessary to obtain correct gauge.

Notions

Crochet hook size US J/10 (6 mm)

Gauge

16 sts and 18 rows = 4" (10 cm) in Malian Lattice Pattern from Chart

Throw

Using A, CO 172 sts. Begin Malian Lattice Pattern from Chart; work sts 1-36 four times, then work sts 1-28 once. Work even until piece measures approximately 62" from the beginning, ending with Row 32 of Chart. Change to A; BO all sts.

Finishing

Crochet Edging: With RS facing, using crochet hook and A, work 2 rnds dc around entire piece, working 3 dc in each corner. Fasten off.
Block lightly (see Special Techniques, page 158).

MALIAN LATTICE PATTERN

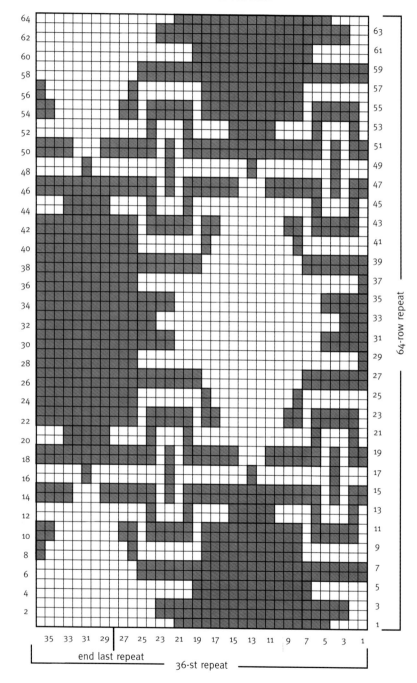

KEY

Knit on RS, purl on WS.

 A

☐ B

64-row repeat

35 33 31 29 27 25 23 21 19 17 15 13 11 9 7 5 3 1

end last repeat

36-st repeat

Kilim

Kilims are handwoven and exuberantly colored tapestries that are commonly used for rugs; they can be found everywhere from Eastern Europe to Southwestern Asia. This two-tone, highly textured afghan is a knitted interpretation of a traditional kilim. Multiple rows of bobbles are worked in a contrasting color for visual punch and are then separated by easy Fair Isle colorwork and garter bands. When working the colorwork, the strands not in use are held to the front, creating the illusion of tapestry weaving.

Finished Measurements
45" wide x 60" long, not including Fringe

Yarn
Berroco Comfort Chunky (50% super fine nylon / 50% super fine acrylic; 100 grams / 150 yards): 10 skeins #5742 Pimpernel (MC); 6 skeins #5741 Bitter Sweet (A)

Needles
One 29" (74 cm) long or longer circular (circ) needle size US 10½ (6.5 mm)
Change needle size if necessary to obtain correct gauge.

Notions
Crochet hook size US J/10 (6 mm)

Gauge
14 sts and 20 rows = 4" (10 cm) in Stockinette stitch (St st)

Abbreviations
MB (make bobble): Knit into front, back, then front of next st to increase to 3 sts, turn; [p1, M1-p] twice, p1, turn; k5, turn; p2tog, p1, p2tog, turn; sk2p–1 st remains.

Throw

Using circ needle and MC, CO 158 sts.

Note: When changing colors, carry color not in use up side edge of work.

Rows 1 and 3 (WS): Purl.

Row 2: Knit.

Row 4: Change to A. Purl.

Row 5: Knit.

Rows 6 and 8: Change to MC. Knit.

Rows 7 and 9: Purl.

Row 10: Change to A. Purl.

Row 11: Knit.

Row 12 and 14: Change to MC. Knit.

Row 13 and 15: Purl.

Row 16: K4 MC, MB A, *k5 MC, MB A; repeat from * to last 3 sts, k3 MC.

Row 17: Change to MC. Purl.

Row 18: Knit.

Row 19: P6 MC, p1 A, *p5 MC, p1 A; repeat from * to last 7 sts, p7 MC.

Row 20: K6 MC, p3 A, *k3 MC, p3 A; repeat from * to last 5 sts, k5 MC.

Row 21: Change to A. Knit.

Row 22: Purl.

Row 23: K5 MC, [p1, k1, p1] A, *k3 MC, [p1, k1, p1] A; repeat from * to last 6 sts, k6 MC.

Row 24: K7 MC, k1 A, *k5 MC, k1 A; repeat from * to last 6 sts, k6 MC.

Row 25: Change to MC. Purl.

Row 26: Knit.

Row 27: *P3 A, p3 MC; repeat from * to last 8 sts, p3 A, p3 MC, p2 A.

Rows 28 and 30: Carrying nonworking yarn across front of work to create floats on RS, p2 A, p3 MC, p3 A, *p3 MC, p3 A; repeat from * to end.

Row 29: Carrying nonworking yarn across back of work to create floats on RS, *k3 A, k3 MC; repeat from * to last 8 sts, k3 A, k3 MC, k2 A.

Row 31: Change to MC. Purl.

Row 32: Knit.

Row 33: Change to A. Knit.

Row 34: Knit.

Repeat Rows 1-34 until piece measures approximately 60" from the beginning, ending with Row 9. BO all sts.

Finishing

Fringe: Cut 10" lengths of each color. Holding 1 strand of each color together, work Fringe along CO and BO edges as follows: Fold strands in half, with RS of piece facing, insert crochet hook just above edge to receive Fringe, from back to front; catch the folded strands of yarn with the hook and pull through work to form a loop, insert ends of yarn through loop and pull to tighten.

Block lightly (see Special Techniques, page 158).

Calico Hill

This knitted afghan takes its cue from a traditional spool pattern design commonly used in American patchwork quilts. It is composed of one shape repeated over and over, and nestled into the shapes around it. When the afghan is finished, gently rounded waves appear at its edges. The solid-colored shapes pop against the multicolored ones, creating a depth and warmth reminiscent of calico prints.

Finished Measurements

47" wide x 62" long

Yarn

Berroco Comfort (50% super fine nylon / 50% super fine acrylic; 100 grams / 210 yards): 5 skeins #9839 Maine Woods (A); 4 skeins each #9759 Duck Teal (B), #9838 Raspberry Tart (C), and #9746 Iron Oxide (D)

Needles

One pair straight needles size US 8 (5 mm)
One 36" (90 cm) long or longer circular (circ) needle size US 8 (5 mm)
Change needle size if necessary to obtain correct gauge.

Notions

Stitch markers

Gauge

18 sts and 24 rows = 4" (10 cm) in 1x2 Rib

Stitch Pattern

1X2 RIB (multiple of 3 sts plus 1; 2-row repeat)
Row 1 (RS): K1, *p2, k1; repeat from * to end.
Row 2: P1, *k2, p1; repeat from * to end.
Repeat Rows 1 and 2 for 1x2 Rib.

Afghan

MOTIF 1 (make 8)
Section 1: Using straight needles and C, CO 45 sts.
Row 1 (WS): Purl.
Row 2: Purl.
Rows 3 and 4: Knit.
Rows 5, 7 and 9: P1, *p1, k5; repeat from * to last 2 sts, p2.
Rows 6 and 8: K1, *k1, p5; repeat from * to last 2 sts, k2.
Row 10: K1, *k1, p1, p2tog, p2; repeat from * to last 2 sts, k2–38 sts remain.

Rows 11, 13, and 15: P1, *p1, k4; repeat from * to last 2 sts, p2.
Rows 12 and 14: K1, *k1, p4; repeat from * to last 2 sts, k2.
Row 16: K1, *k1, p1, p2tog, p1; repeat from * to last 2 sts, k2–31 sts remain.
Rows 17, 19 and 21: P1, *p1, k3; repeat from * to last 2 sts, p2.
Rows 18 and 20: K1, *k1, p3; repeat from * to last 2 sts, k2.
Row 22: K1, *k1, p1, p2tog; repeat from * to last 2 sts, k2–24 sts remain.
Rows 23 and all WS Rows through Row 37: P1, *p1, k2; repeat from * to last 2 sts, p2.
Rows 24 and all RS Rows through Row 38: K1, *k1, p2; repeat from * to last 2 sts, k2.
Row 39: P1, *p1, k1, M1, k1; repeat from * to last 2 sts, p2 – 31 sts.
Rows 40, 42 and 44: K1, *k1, p3; repeat from * to last 2 sts, k2.
Rows 41 and 43: P1, *p1, k3; repeat from * to last 2 sts, p2.
Row 45: P1, *p1, k1, M1, k2; repeat from * to last 2 sts, p2–38 sts.
Rows 46, 48 and 50: K1, *k1, p4; repeat from * to last 2 sts, k2.
Rows 47 and 49: P1, *p1, k4; repeat from * to last 2 sts, p2.
Row 51: P1, *p1, k2, M1, k2; repeat from * to last 2 sts, p2–45 sts.
Rows 52, 54 and 56: K1, *k1, p5; repeat from * to last 2 sts, k2.
Rows 53 and 55: P1, *p1, k5; repeat from * to last 2 sts, p2.
Rows 57 and 58: Purl.
Rows 59 and 60: Knit.
Row 61: Purl.
BO all sts.

Section 2: With RS of Section 1 facing, using D, pick up and knit 45 sts evenly spaced along right-hand edge of Section 1. Complete as for Section 1.
Section 3: With RS of Section 2 facing, using A, pick up and knit 45 sts evenly spaced along right-hand edge of Section 2. Complete as for Section 1.
Section 4: With RS of Section 3 facing, using B, pick up and knit 45 sts evenly spaced along right-hand edge of Section 3. Complete as for Section 1.
Sew top of Section 1 to left-hand side of Section 4.

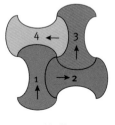

Motif 1

knitting direction

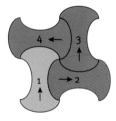

Motif 2

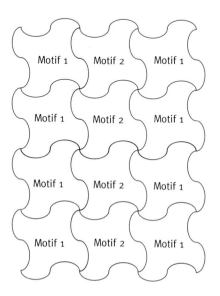

MOTIF 2 (make 4)

Section 1: Using straight needles and B, CO 45 sts. Work as for Section 1 of Motif 1.

Section 2: With RS of Section 1 facing, using A, pick up and knit 45 sts evenly spaced along right-hand edge of Section 1. Complete as for Section 1.

Section 3: With RS of Section 2 facing, using D, pick up and knit 45 sts evenly spaced along right-hand edge of Section 2. Complete as for Section 1.

Section 4: With RS of Section 3 facing, using C, pick up and knit 45 sts evenly spaced along right-hand edge of Section 3. Complete as for Section 1.

Sew top of Section 1 to left-hand side of Section 4.

Finishing

Sew Motifs 1 and 2 together following Assembly Diagram.

Bottom Border: With RS facing, using circ needle and A, and beginning at lower right-hand corner of Motif 1, *pick up and knit 42 sts evenly spaced along first color Section, place marker (pm), pick up and knit 48 sts evenly spaced along next color section, pm, placing markers each side of center 6 sts in this Section; repeat from * twice–270 sts. Knit 1 row.

Decrease Row (RS): *K42, knit to 2 sts before first center marker on next color Section, ssk, slip marker (sm), k6, sm, k2tog, knit to end of Section; repeat from * twice. Knit 1 row. Repeat last 2 rows twice–252 sts remain. BO all sts.

Top Border: Work as for Bottom Border on opposite edge.

Side Border: With RS facing, using circ needle and A, pick up and knit 5 sts from Bottom Border, *pick up and knit 42 sts evenly spaced along first color Section, pm, pick up and knit 48 sts evenly spaced along next color Section, placing markers each side of center 6 sts in this Section; repeat from * 3 times, pick up 5 sts from Top Border–370 sts. Complete as for Bottom Border. BO remaining 228 sts. Repeat for opposite side. Block lightly (see Special Techniques, page 158).

Herringbone

Cables and twisted stitches are used in combination to create this simple herringbone twill adaptation. The pattern is easy to memorize, making this a perfect project to work on during long hours of conversation in front of a cozy fire. If you are new to cables, this is a good project with which to start.

Finished Measurements
46" wide x 59" long

Yarn
Berroco Comfort (50% super fine nylon / 50% super fine acrylic; 100 grams / 210 yards): 11 skeins #9781 Olive

Needles
One 36" (90 cm) long or longer circular (circ) needle size US 9 (5.5 mm)
Change needle size if necessary to obtain correct gauge.

Notions
Crochet hook size US H/8 (5 mm); cable needle (cn)

Gauge
18 sts and 24 rows = 4" (10 cm) in Herringbone Pattern from Chart

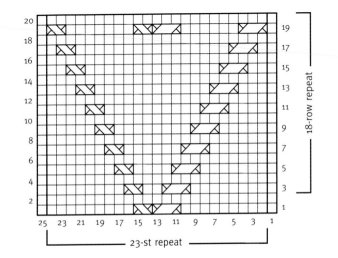

HERRINGBONE PATTERN

23-st repeat

18-row repeat

KEY

☐ Knit on RS, purl on WS.

▱ Slip next st to cn, hold to back, k2, k1 from cn.

▨ Knit into back of second st, then knit first and second sts together through back loop, slip both sts from left-hand needle together.

Throw
Using circ needle, CO 209 sts. Begin Herringbone Pattern from Chart; work Rows 1 and 2 once, then work Rows 3-20 until piece measures approximately 58" from the beginning, ending with Row 20 of Chart. BO all sts.

Finishing
CROCHET EDGING
Rnd 1: With RS facing, using crochet hook, join yarn with slip st in any corner, ch 1, work sc around entire throw, working 3 sc in each corner, join with sl st in ch.
Rnd 2: Ch 1, working from left to right, work Reverse sc around entire throw, working 3 Reverse sc in each corner, join with sl st in ch.
Block lightly (see Special Techniques, page 158).

Incline

This afghan is worked in three long strips, each composed by alternating three stitches—garter stitch, stockinette, and lacy short rows. The sides of each strip are finished with garter stitch, and then the strips are sewn together. The result is a textured fabric with an interesting combination of triangular inclines and solid spaces.

Finished Measurements

53" wide x 58" long

Yarn

Berroco Comfort (50% super fine nylon / 50% super fine acrylic; 100 grams / 210 yards): 13 skeins #9757 Lillet

Needles

One pair straight needles size US 8 (5 mm)
One pair straight needles size US 9 (5.5 mm)
One 29" (74 cm) long or longer circular (circ) needle US 8 (5 mm)
Change needle size if necessary to obtain correct gauge.

Gauge

17 sts and 26 rows = 4" (10 cm) in Stockinette stitch (St st), using larger needles

Stitch Pattern

WEDGE STITCH (70 sts; 20 rows)
Rows 1 and 2: [Yo, p2tog] 32 times, turn.
Rows 3 and 4: [Yo, p2tog] 29 times, turn.
Rows 5 and 6: [Yo, p2tog] 26 times, turn
Rows 7 and 8: [Yo, p2tog] 23 times, turn.
Rows 9 and 10: [Yo, p2tog] 20 times, turn.
Rows 11 and 12: [Yo, p2tog] 17 times, turn.
Rows 13 and 14: [Yo, p2tog] 14 times, turn.
Rows 15 and 16: [Yo, p2tog] 11 times, turn.
Rows 17 and 18: [Yo, p2tog] 8 times, turn.
Rows 19 and 20: [Yo, p2tog] 5 times, turn.

Afghan

STRIP (make 3)
Using smaller needles, CO 70 sts.
Rows 1 (RS)-6: Knit.
Rows 7-26: Work Wedge St.
Rows 27-32: Knit.
Row 33-49: Change to larger needles. Work in St st, beginning with a knit row.
Rows 50-55: Change to smaller needles. Knit.
Rows 56-75: Work Wedge St.
Rows 76-81: Knit.
Rows 82-98: Change to larger needles. Work in St st, beginning with a purl row.
Repeat Rows 1-98 five times, then repeat Rows 1-32 once. BO all sts.

Finishing

Edging: With RS facing, using circ needle, pick up and knit 270 sts evenly spaced along each side of each Strip. Begin Garter St (knit every row); work even for ¾". BO all sts.
Lay 3 Strips next to each other, so that the outside Strips have BO ends at the top and the center Strip has its BO end at the bottom. Sew Strips together.
Block lightly (see Special Techniques, page 158).

Flokati

This throw was inspired by *flokati* rugs from Greece. These traditional wool floor coverings, which date back to the fifth century, are woven and then rinsed in turbulent mountain streams to draw out huge amounts of fluff. Our modern interpretation is worked in a looped stitch. We chose a natural shade of yarn, reminiscent of black sheep's wool, but you may prefer a bright, solid color for futuristic appeal.

Finished Measurements

45" wide x 60" long

Yarn

Berroco Comfort (50% super fine nylon / 50% super fine acrylic; 100 grams / 210 yards): 18 skeins #9741 Bitter Sweet

Needles

One 36" (90 cm) long or longer circular (circ) needle size US 8 (5 mm)
Change needle size if necessary to obtain correct gauge.

Gauge

16 sts and 32 rows = 4" (10 cm) in Loop Stitch

Stitch Pattern

LOOP STITCH (any number of sts; 6-row repeat)
Rows 1 (WS)-4: Knit.
Row 5: *Holding third finger of left hand over yarn behind work, k1, looping yarn around finger; do not remove finger from st or drop st from right-hand needle, transfer st just worked back onto left-hand needle and k2tog-tbl (st just worked together with original st); removing finger from loop, pull loop tightly to RS; repeat from * to end.
Row 6: *K1-tbl; repeat from * to end.
Repeat Rows 1-6 for Loop Stitch.

Throw

CO 180 sts. Begin Loop st; work even until piece measures approximately 60" from the beginning, ending with Row 4 of pattern. BO all sts.

Finishing

Block lightly (see Special Techniques, page 158).

Maine

This colorful afghan is made of striped squares that are worked individually and then sewn together at the end. We chose colors in multiple shades of the same hue for each square, then arranged them into large checks akin to buffalo plaid. To add complexity, some of the stripes meet at perpendicular angles, while others unexpectedly run parallel.

Finished Measurements

45" wide x 63" long

Yarn

Berroco Comfort (50% super fine nylon / 50% super fine acrylic; 100 grams / 210 yards): 2 skeins each #9761 Lovage (A), #9809 Antipasto Mix (B), #9762 Spruce (C), #9741 Bitter Sweet (D), #9747 Cadet (H), and #9739 Grape Jelly (I); 1 skein each #9760 Beet Root (E), #9745 Filbert (F), #9724 Pumpkin (G), #9763 Navy Blue (J), #9720 Hummus (K), #9743 Goldenrod (L), and #9712 Buttercup (M)

Crochet Hook

Crochet hook size US G/6 (4 mm)
Change hook size if necessary to obtain correct gauge.

Gauge

16 sts and 8 rows = 4" (10 cm) in Double Crochet (dc)

Afghan

SQUARE 1 (make 10)
Using A, ch 38.
Row 1 (RS): Dc in 4th ch from hook and in each ch across–36 sts, turn.
Row 2: Ch 3 (counts as dc), sk 1st dc, dc in each dc across, turn.
Row 3: Using B, ch 3 (counts as dc), sk 1st dc, dc in the back loop of each dc across, turn.
Row 4: Using B, ch 3 (counts as dc), sk 1st dc, dc in each dc across, turn.
Rows 5 and 6: Using C, repeat Rows 3 and 4.
Rows 7 and 8: Using A, repeat rows 3 and 4.
Rows 9-18: Repeat Rows 3-8 once, then Rows 3-6 once. Fasten off.

SQUARE 2 (make 10)
Using D, ch 38.
Row 1 (RS): Dc in 4th ch from hook and in each ch across–36 sts, turn.
Row 2: Using E, ch 3 (counts as dc), sk 1st dc, dc in the front loop of each dc across, turn.
Row 3: Using F, ch 3 (counts as dc), sk 1st dc, dc in the back loop of each dc across, turn.
Row 4: Using G, ch 3 (counts as dc), sk 1st dc, dc in the front loop of each dc across, turn.
Row 5: Using D, ch 3 (counts as dc), sk 1st dc, dc in the back loop of each dc across, turn.
Rows 6-18: Repeat Rows 2-5 three times, then repeat Row 2 once. Fasten off.

ASSEMBLY DIAGRAM

SQUARE 2 ←	SQUARE 1 ↑	SQUARE 2 ←	SQUARE 1 ↑	SQUARE 2 ←
SQUARE 4 ←	SQUARE 3 ↑	SQUARE 4 ←	SQUARE 3 ↑	SQUARE 4 ←
SQUARE 1 ↑	SQUARE 2 ←	SQUARE 1 ↑	SQUARE 2 ←	SQUARE 1 ↑
SQUARE 3 ↑	SQUARE 4 ←	SQUARE 3 ↑	SQUARE 4 ←	SQUARE 3 ↑
SQUARE 2 ←	SQUARE 1 ↑	SQUARE 2 ←	SQUARE 1 ↑	SQUARE 2 ←
SQUARE 4 ←	SQUARE 3 ↑	SQUARE 4 ←	SQUARE 3 ↑	SQUARE 4 ←
SQUARE 1 ↑	SQUARE 2 ←	SQUARE 1 ↑	SQUARE 2 ←	SQUARE 1 ↑

crochet direction

SQUARE 3 (make 7)

Using H, ch 38.

Row 1 (RS): Dc in 4th ch from hook and in each ch across–36 sts, turn.

Row 2: Using I, ch 3 (counts as dc), sk 1st dc, dc in front loop of each dc across, turn.

Row 3: Using I, ch 3 (counts as dc), sk 1st dc, dc in each dc across, turn.

Rows 4 and 5: Using J, repeat Rows 2 and 3.

Rows 6: Using H, repeat Row 2.

Row 7: Using I, ch 3 (counts as dc), sk 1st dc, dc in each dc across, turn.

Row 8: Using I, ch 3 (counts as dc), sk 1st dc, dc in front loop of each dc across, turn.

Rows 9 and 10: Using J, repeat Rows 7 and 8.

Row 11: Using H, repeat Row 3.

Rows 12-18: Repeat Rows 2-8. Fasten off.

SQUARE 4 (make 8)

Using K, ch 38.

Row 1 (RS): Dc in 4th ch from hook and in each ch across–36 sts, turn.

Row 2: Ch 3 (counts as dc), sk 1st dc, dc in each dc across, turn.

Row 3: Using L, ch 3 (counts as dc), sk 1st dc, dc in the back loop of each dc across, turn.

Row 4: Using M, ch 3 (counts as dc), sk 1st dc, dc in the front loop of each dc across, turn.

Row 5: Using M, ch 3 (counts as dc), sk 1st dc, dc in the back loop of each dc across, turn.

Rows 6 and 7: Using K, repeat Rows 4 and 5.

Row 8: Using L, repeat Row 4.

Rows 9 and 10: Using M, repeat Rows 3 and 4.

Row 11 and 12: Using K, repeat Rows 3 and 4.

Rows 13-18: Repeat Rows 3-8. Fasten off.

Finishing

Sew Squares together following Assembly Diagram.

Block lightly (see Special Techniques, page 158).

Aran

In this textured afghan, cables twist, intertwine, and weave together to form an elaborate motif reminiscent of the traditional sweaters of the Aran Islands. With careful attention to the chart, you will find that this one's not as complex as it looks. The trick? We alternated the starting points of the cables within each column.

Finished Measurements
53" wide x 64" long

Yarn
Berroco Comfort (50% super fine nylon / 50% super fine acrylic; 100 grams / 210 yards): 15 skeins #9720 Hummus

Needles
One 36" (90 cm) long or longer circular (circ) needle size US 8 (5 mm)
Change needle size if necessary to obtain correct gauge.

Notions
Cable needle (cn); stitch markers

Gauge
24 sts and 26 rows = 4" (10 cm) in cable pattern from Chart B or C

Afghan
CO 307 sts.
Begin Pattern (WS): Work 6 sts in Garter st (knit every row), place marker (pm), *work 5 sts from Chart A, pm, 24 sts from Chart B, pm, 5 sts from Chart A, pm, 24 sts from Chart C, pm; repeat from * 4 times more, pm, work 5 sts from Chart A, pm, work 6 sts in Garter st. Work even until piece measures approximately 64" from beginning, ending with Row 11 or 21 of Chart B. BO all sts.

Finishing
Block lightly (see Special Techniques, page 158).

CHART A

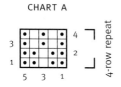

CHART B

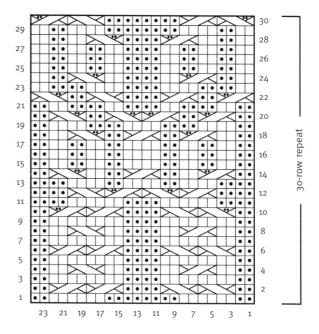

30-row repeat

KEY

☐ Knit on RS, purl on WS.

• Purl on RS, knit on WS.

 Slip 2 sts to cn, hold to back, k2, k2 from cn.

Slip 2 sts to cn, hold to front, k2, k2 from cn.

Slip 2 sts to cn, hold to back, k2, p2 from cn.

Slip 2 sts to cn, hold to front, k2, p2 from cn.

CHART C

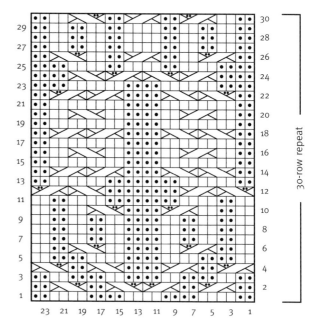

30-row repeat

Sunny Day

Stripes seem to define summer—from beach accessories like towels, blankets, and umbrellas, to outdoor furnishings like awnings, hammocks, and chair pads. Taking its cue from these summer standards, this afghan is crocheted in a combination of blues, greens, and complementary oranges with the added surprise of a variegated yarn for a pleasing, dappled effect.

Finished Measurements
45" wide x 55" long

Yarn
Berroco Comfort (50% super fine nylon / 50% super fine acrylic; 100 grams / 210 yards): 3 skeins each #9703 Barley (A), #9756 Copen Blue (B), #9761 Lovage (E), and #9830 Antipasto (F); 2 skeins each #9743 Goldenrod (C), #9724 Pumpkin (D), and #9725 Dutch Teal (G)

Crochet Hook
Crochet hook size US I/9 (5.5 mm)
Change hook size if necessary to obtain correct gauge.

Gauge
15 sts and 13 rows = 4" (10 cm) in Stripe Pattern

Stitch Pattern
STRIPE PATTERN (any number of sts + 1 ch; 10 row repeat).
Set-Up Row (RS): Sc in 2nd ch from hook and in each ch across–210 sc.
Row 1: Ch 1, sc in each sc across, turn.
Row 2: Change to B. Ch 3 (counts as dc), skip first sc and work dc in each sc across, turn.
Row 3: Change to C. Ch 1, sc in each dc across, turn.
Row 4: Change to D. Ch 2 (counts as hdc), skip first sc, work hdc in each sc across, turn.
Row 5: Change to E. Ch 3 (counts as dc), skip first hdc and work dc in each hdc across, turn.
Rows 6-8: Change to F. Ch 1, sc in each dc across, turn.
Row 9: Change to G. Ch 1, sc in each sc across, turn.
Row 10: Change to A. Ch 1, sc in each sc across, turn.
Repeat Rows 1-10 for Stripe Pattern.

Throw
Using A, ch 211.
Begin Stripe Pattern; work even until piece measures 45" from the beginning. Fasten off.

Finishing
Block lightly (see Special Techniques, page 158).

SPECIAL TECHNIQUES
& ABBREVIATIONS

Special Techniques

knit

GARTER STITCH

Knit every row when working straight; knit 1 round, purl 1 round when working circular.

INTARSIA COLORWORK METHOD

Use a separate length of yarn for each color section; you may wind yarn onto bobbins to make color changes easier. When changing colors, bring the new yarn up and to the right of the yarn just used to twist the yarns and prevent leaving a hole; do not carry colors not in use across the back of the work.

READING CHARTS

Unless otherwise specified in the instructions, when working straight, charts are read from right to left for RS rows, and from left to right for WS rows. Row numbers are written at the beginning of each row. Numbers on the right indicate RS rows; numbers on the left indicate WS rows. When working circular, all rounds are read from right to left.

REVERSE STOCKINETTE STITCH (REV ST ST)

Purl on RS rows, knit on WS rows when working straight; purl every round when working circular.

STOCKINETTE STITCH (ST ST)

Knit on RS rows, purl on WS rows when working straight; knit every round when working circular.

STRANDED (FAIR ISLE) COLORWORK METHOD

When more than one color is used per row, carry color(s) not in use loosely across the WS of work. Be sure to secure all colors at beginning and end of rows to prevent holes.

YARN OVER (YO) OTHER THAN BEGINNING OF ROW

Bring yarn forward (to the purl position), then place it in position to work the next st. If next st is to be knit, bring yarn over the needle and knit; if next st is to be purled, bring yarn over the needle and then forward again to the purl position and purl. Work the yarnover in pattern on the next row unless instructed otherwise.

crochet

CROCHET CHAIN

Make a slip knot and place it on the crochet hook. Holding tail end of yarn in left hand, *take hook under ball end of yarn from front to back; draw yarn on hook back through previous st on hook to form new st. Repeat from * to desired number of sts or length of chain.

embroidery

BOUILLION STITCH

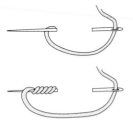

CROSS STITCH

4 2
1 3

OVERCAST ST

CHAIN STITCH

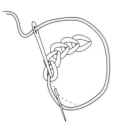

LAZY DAISY EMBROIDERY STITCH

ROUMANIAN STITCH

A

B

Special Techniques

embroidery

STEM STITCH

STRAIGHT STITCH

blocking

To flatten seams or neaten the overall look of an afghan, dampen the piece slightly with water from a spray bottle or with a damp cloth, finger press affected areas, and lay flat to dry.

When a more serious blocking is needed, pin the piece to size on a flat surface, place a damp towel (or towels) on top, and let dry.

Abbreviations

crochet

Ch Chain

Dc (Double crochet) Yarn over hook (2 loops on hook), insert hook into next st, yarn over hook and and pull up a loop (3 loops on hook), [yarn over and draw through 2 loops] twice.

Dc-tog (Double crochet together) Yarn over hook (2 loops on hook), insert hook into the next st, yarn over hook and pull up a loop (3 loops on hook), yarn and draw through 2 loops on hook, yarn over hook (3 loops on hook), insert hook into next st, yarn over hook and pull up a loop (4 loops on hook), yarn over hook and draw through 2 loops on hook, yarn over hook and draw yarn through 3 loops on hook.

Hdc (Half double crochet) Yarn over hook (2 loops on hook), insert hook into next st, yarn over hook and pull up a loop (3 loops on hook), yarn over hook and draw through 3 loops on hook.

MB Make bobble.

Reverse sc (Reverse single crochet) Working from right to left, insert hook into next st to the right, yarn over hook and pull up a loop (2 loops on hook), yarn over hook and draw through 2 loops on hook.

Rnd(s) Round(s)

Sc (Single crochet) Insert hook into next st, yarn over hook and pull up a loop (2 loops on hook), yarn over hook and draw through 2 loops on hook.

Sk Skip.

Sl Slip.

Sp Space

St(s) Stitch(es)

Tr (Triple crochet) Yarn over hook twice (3 loops on hook), insert hook into next st, yarn over hook and pull up a loop (4 loops on hook), [yarn over hook and draw through 2 loops on hook] 3 times.

Yo Yarn over

knit

BO Bind off.

CO Cast on.

Circ Circular

Cn Cable needle

Dpn(s) Double-pointed needle(s)

K Knit.

K1-f/b Knit into front loop and back loop of same stitch to increase 1 stitch.

K2tog Knit 2 together.

K2tog-tbl Knit 2 together through back loops.

M1-l (Make 1 left-slanting) With tip of left-hand needle inserted from front to back, lift strand between 2 needles onto left-hand needle; knit strand through back loop to increase 1 st.

M1-p (make 1 purlwise) With tip of left-hand needle inserted from back to front, lift strand between 2 needles onto left-hand needle; purl strand through front loop to increase 1 stitch.

M1-r (make 1 right-slanting) With tip of left-hand needle inserted from back to front, lift strand between 2 needles onto left-hand needle; knit it through front loop to increase 1 stitch.

MB Make bobble.

MC Main color

P Purl.

P2tog Purl 2 together.

P2tog-tbl Purl 2 together through back loops.

Pm Place marker.

Rnd(s) Round(s)

RS Right side

Sk2p Slip 1, k2 together, pass slipped st over knit st.

Sl Slip.

Ssk (slip, slip, knit) Slip 2 sts to right-hand needle one at a time as if to knit; return them back to left-hand needle one at a time in their new orientation; knit them together through the back loops.

St(s) Stitch(es)

St st (Stockinette stitch) Knit on RS, purl on WS.

Tbl Through the back loop

Wyib With yarn in back

Wyif With yarn in front

WS Wrong side

Yo Yarn over

History of Berroco

When Warren Wheelock's great-great-great-grandfather opened the first of the Wheelock Mills in rural Massachusetts in 1810, he began a dynamic enterprise that has endured over six generations. Beginning as Stanley Woolen Mills, the firm survived two depressions, weathering changing times and evolving demands in the world of textiles. In 1968, the Wheelock family formed a new hand-knitting subsidiary. This new firm grew to become one of the largest importers and wholesalers of hand-knitting yarns and patterns to independent yarn shops in the United States and Canada. Operating on the site of one of the Wheelock family's original woolen mills, Berroco, Inc., continues the family tradition of changing with the needs of the times to provide top-quality products.

Comfort Yarn

All of the yarns in *Comfort Knitting & Crochet: Afghans* were made with Berroco Comfort, which is available in worsted, dk, and chunky weights in more than 95 shades. In order to view Comfort shade cards, find a store, or for any other information, visit www.berroco.com or email info@berroco.com.

www.berroco.com

Design Credits

The Berroco Design Team worked together on many of the afghans in this collection, and at other times worked on projects individually. Following are credits for designs worked on by individuals:

Norah Gaughan: Aran, Bright Star, Calico Hill, Crazy, Floret, Herringbone, Incline, Mindful, Nordic Holiday, Petal, Retro, Spiral, Swirl, Textured Knots, Weave
Cirilia Rose: Vintage
Margery Winter: Basketweave, Danish Modern, Fish Ripples, Flokati, Garter Stripes, Gypsy Patchwork, Houndstooth, Kilim, Lucy, Malian Lattice, Mistletoe, Pinwheel, Stella, Still Life, Seersucker, Trapper, Ukrainian Tiles, Westchester Winter, ZigZag
Donna Yacino: Bicolor Chevron, Dots, Ethel, Greenway, Irish Floral, Marrakesh, Meditate, Ribbon, Serpentine, Simplicity
Brenda York: Autumn Haze, Little Waves, Maine, Square Off, Stripe by Stripe, Sunny Day

Acknowledgments

While Margery Winter and Norah Gaughan are the primary authors of this volume, it is with gratitude that they acknowledge the contributions of the other members of the Berroco Design Team. Brenda York and Donna Yacino shared their ideas and expertise and, in the process, influenced and improved many of the designs. Cirilia Rose and Amanda Keep rounded out the team with their finishing skills and attention to detail. The many sample knitters and crocheters were also integral to the process, generously sharing much-needed insight and encouragement as they brought each afghan to life, stitch by stitch. Lastly, this book would not be possible without the pattern-writing skills and persistence of our technical editor, Barbara Khouri, for whom we have great appreciation.